New Jersey

New Jersey

R. Conrad Stein

Children's Press®
A Division of Grolier Publishing
New York   London   Hong Kong   Sydney
Danbury, Connecticut

Frontispiece: Autumn at High Point State Park
Front cover: Barnegat Lighthouse, the Jersey Shore
Back cover: The Palisades of New Jersey

Consultant: Robert E. Lupp, New Jersey State Library

Please note: All statistics are as up-to-date as possible at the time of publication.

Visit Children's Press on the Internet at http://publishing.grolier.com

Book production by Editorial Directions, Inc.

Library of Congress Cataloging-in-Publication Data

Stein, R. Conrad.
    New Jersey / by R. Conrad Stein.
      p. cm. — (America the beautiful. Second series)
    Includes bibliographical references and index.
    Summary : Describes the geography, plants, animals, history, economy,
  religions, culture, sports, arts, and people of the Garden State.
    ISBN 0-516-20637-0
    1. New Jersey—Juvenile literature. [1. New Jersey.] I. Title. II. Series.
  F134.3.S74 1998
  974.9—dc21   97-41839
                                                                                  CIP
                                                                                   AC

To my wife's family, the Kents:
Doris, Gordon, Gordon Jr., Zachary, and Connie—all of
them solid citizens of New Jersey, the Garden State

The Delaware
Water Gap

Newport Marina

Cape May

Contents

Bruce Springsteen

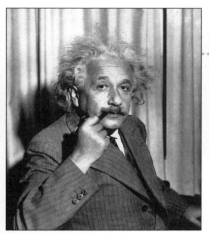

Albert Einstein

Island Beach State Park

George Washington Bridge

Monopoly game pieces

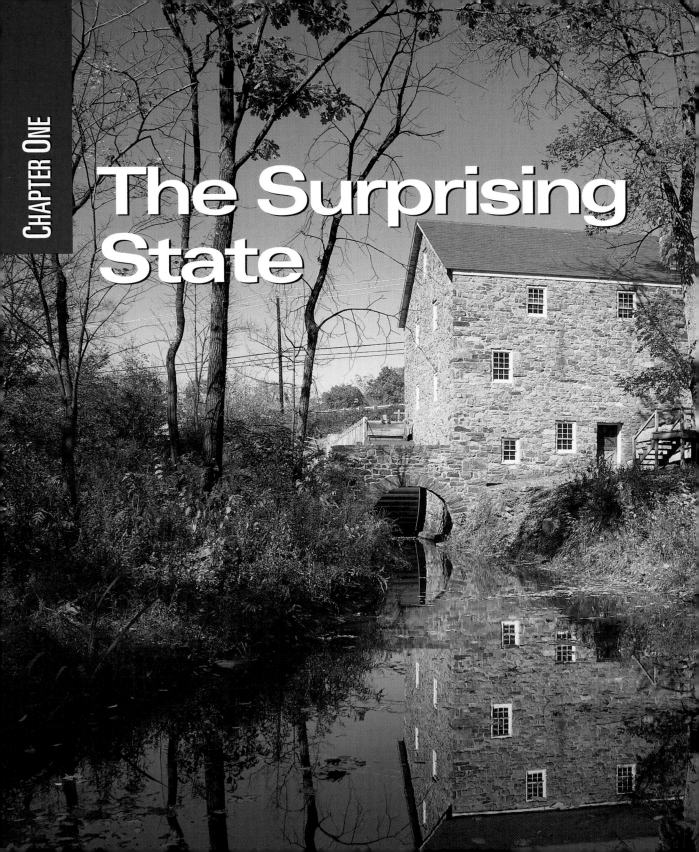

CHAPTER ONE

The Surprising State

EXITS 14-14A-14B-14C
78 1 2
Newark Airport
Holland Tunnel

EXITS 14-14 A-14B-14C 1 MI
78 1 9 22
Newark Airport
Holland Tunnel

SHOULDER
CLOSED

Take a drive on the New Jersey Turnpike. It is the busiest road in the United States, and thousands of cars crowd onto it each day. It is also the country's widest road, bulging up to twelve lanes in some stretches. The New Jersey Turnpike is the major thoroughfare between New York City and Philadelphia. Many people traveling between the two cities zip through New Jersey without getting off the roadway. Sadly, this is the traveler's loss as well as the state's lament. Americans too often think of New Jersey as just a passageway between other places. Glued to the road, they fail to see New Jersey as the beautiful and fascinating state it really is.

Delightful surprises await those who explore New Jersey's cities, towns, parks, beaches, and farmland. This is a small state, squeezed between the Delaware River and the Atlantic Ocean—only Rhode Island, Connecticut, Delaware, and Hawaii are smaller.

The New Jersey Turnpike is a major thoroughfare.

Opposite:
A historic mill in Chester

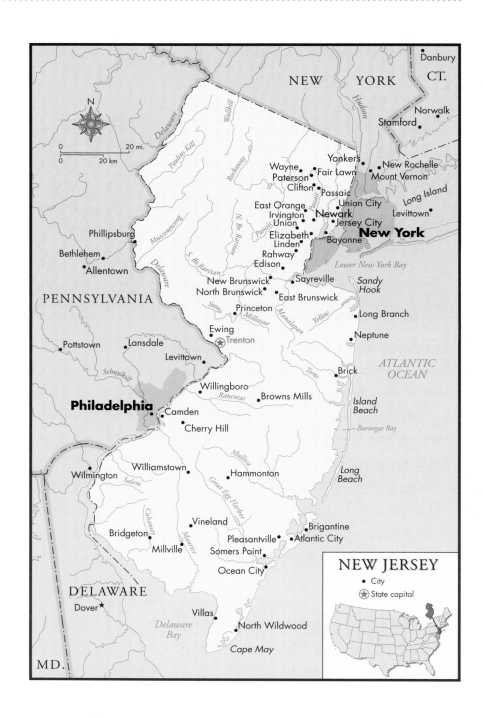

**Geopolitical map
of New Jersey**

Yet New Jersey holds almost 8 million people, ranking as America's ninth most populous state. So many people packed into such a small area means that New Jersey is terribly overcrowded, right? Wrong! About two-thirds of the state's land is covered by forests or farmland. In the north lie scores of sparkling lakes. Along the Delaware River to the west spread the fertile farms that have given New Jersey its nickname, the Garden State. To the east stretch the silvery beaches of New Jersey's famous Atlantic shore. And in the middle of the state stand the Pine Barrens, 1,000 square miles (2,590 sq km) of wilderness.

Throughout history, New Jersey has contributed to America's success. New Jersey was one of the thirteen original English colonies, and nearly 100 battles were fought on its soil during the Revolutionary War. The state has produced two presidents, and world-famous scientists and inventors such as Thomas Edison and Albert Einstein did their most productive work here.

Despite its natural beauty and its soaring achievements, New Jersey remains a maligned state in the minds of many Americans. To some, it is little more than a spider's web of highways. Others see it as a collection of suburbs from which people rush to work in New York City and Philadelphia. New York nightclub comedians delight in telling "Jersey jokes." Brendan Byrne, New Jersey's governor from 1974 to 1982, once said, "The state between the Liberty Bell and the Statue of Liberty has suffered because of its location. New Jersey has been called a state without an ego—a corridor between New York City and Philadelphia."

But those who see the state as a corridor miss its surprises. They miss chatting with its friendly people. They miss browsing in its

interesting museums and art galleries. They miss the scrumptious food served in its roadside diners—New Jersey institutions. A host of wonders await those who exit the New Jersey Turnpike. New Jersey has long been called the Garden State, but perhaps an even better nickname would be the Surprising State.

New Jersey's bountiful farms are among the state's hidden treasures.

CHAPTER TWO

Origins of the Garden State

At the time Europeans touched upon New Jersey's shores, about 8,000 Indians lived in what is now the Garden State. The majority belonged to the Lenni-Lenape tribe. Lenni-Lenape means "genuine people" and is sometimes translated as "original people." Of course the Lenni-Lenape were not the original inhabitants of New Jersey. Human settlement in the state dates back at least 10,000 years. Little is known about New Jersey's ancient residents, but historians have learned about the Lenni-Lenape and their unique society.

Life Among the Lenni-Lenape

Legends claim that the Lenni-Lenape came from the north, probably from what is now Canada. The people migrated south until they reached what they called the "salt sea"—the Atlantic Ocean. European colonists later called the Lenni-Lenape "the Delaware" because many of their villages lay along the Delaware River.

During the Lenni-Lenape era, New Jersey was a land of towering forests—the woodlands home of deer, elk, bear, and many other animals. Its rivers and lakes teemed with fish, as did its ocean waters. We might imagine that New Jersey was a Garden of

One of the Lenni-Lenape people

Opposite: A New Jersey rose garden

Most Lenni-Lenape villages lay along the Delaware River.

Eden for the Lenni-Lenape people, but their legends spoke of an older and even more enchanting land.

We know this because the Lenni-Lenape once wrote a creation myth on a piece of tree bark. That bark, which still exists, is called the *Walum Olum,* which means "painted records." The *Walum Olum* contains a story remarkably similar to the one told in first chapter of the Bible. According to the story, the supreme creator, Manito, "made the sun, the moon, and the stars. He made them all move evenly." The legend goes on to say that an evil snake once lived among the Lenni-Lenape and caused the people to argue and lie to each other. Because of this dissension, the Lenni-Lenape had to leave their marvelous homeland in the north. For years, they wandered in the wilderness before finding their second home, in New Jersey.

The Lenni-Lenape were an industrious people who thrived by farming, hunting, and fishing. They sailed through the state's many rivers in sturdy dugout canoes, some large enough to hold twenty people. They cut trails through the forests that led from villages to hunting and fishing grounds. A half-dozen major trails crossed the entire width of present-day New Jersey. Along Atlantic Ocean beaches, the Lenni-Lenape gathered oysters, clams, and other shellfish. They dried the meat of the fish and piled the shells in great mounds. Hundreds of years later, New Jersey farmers discovered these mounds and ground up the shells for fertilizer.

The Lenni-Lenape made dugout canoes to travel through their rivers.

Lenni-Lenape villages were a collection of roundhouses, one for each family. The houses were made by cutting young trees, placing them in the ground to form a circle, and tying the tops together. This frame was then covered with tree bark and grass. Usually a hole was left at the top to allow smoke to escape from a cooking fire.

A religious people, the Lenni-Lenape worshiped a supreme creator along with a host of lesser gods and spirits. They loved music and dance, and storytelling was one of their passions. They were fierce fighters when attacked. Early French travelers called the Lenni-Lenape "wolves" because their warriors were fearless. But for the most part, the Lenni-Lenape greeted strangers in the spirit of friendship, and peace prevailed in their lands. One of their most important tribal traditions was keeping a pot full of food simmering on the fire for unexpected guests.

Abbott Farm

In 1872, pottery, stone knives, and other traces of New Jersey's ancient people were unearthed at the Abbott Farm near Trenton. These objects, made centuries ago by human hands, are now displayed at the New Jersey State Museum. The Abbott Farm artifacts are believed to be more than 2,000 years old. ◼

Giovanni da Verrazano

Explorers and Colonists

An Italian sea captain named Giovanni da Verrazano was probably the first European to see the coast of New Jersey. Sailing in the service of France, he arrived off the New Jersey shore in 1524 and dropped anchor at the stem of land now called Sandy Hook. The captain was impressed by the groups of curious Lenni-Lenape who climbed aboard his ship. He wrote, "They came without fear aboard our ship. This is the goodliest people and of the fairest conditions that we have found in this our voyage."

The famous explorer Henry Hudson (Hudson Bay and the Hudson River are named in his honor) entered Newark Bay in 1609. For unknown reasons, his party clashed with the Lenni-Lenape. One of Hudson's officers, killed by an Indian arrow,

Blessed Are the Peacemakers

The Lenni-Lenape had a saying: "Kill the snake that gives no warning before it bites; spare the one that gives warning." The saying describes their live-and-let-live attitude toward neighbors. They were so peaceful that rival Indian groups sometimes denounced them as cowards. But when nearby tribes were on the brink of war, they called upon Lenni-Lenape negotiators to help reach a settlement. Lenni-Lenape peacemakers saved hundreds of lives over the years.

became the first recorded casualty of what would be a bloody series of Indian wars fought on the east coast of the United States. In 1614, the Dutch explorer Cornelius Mey sailed into the mouth of the Delaware River and built a tiny fort near what is now the town of Gloucester. Cape May, at the southern tip of the state, is named after him.

The Dutch claimed a huge tract of land that included parts of New York and New Jersey. They called the area New Netherland. Dutch traders established an outpost in what is now Jersey City in 1630. The forests of New Netherland were rich with fur-bearing animals—fox, mink, otter, and beaver. The pelts of these animals were used to make fashionable hats and scarves in Europe, and they were considered very valuable. Indians trapped the animals and traded the pelts to the Dutch for European goods such as iron kettles, firearms, and rum.

Swedes also came to New Netherland to participate in the profitable fur trade. The first log cabins erected in the United States were built by Swedish immigrants on New Jersey soil. Years later, when the nation expanded westward, the log cabin became a symbol of the frontier. For a few years, the Dutch and the Swedes fought over territory. But the greatest threat to Dutch power in New Netherland came from England.

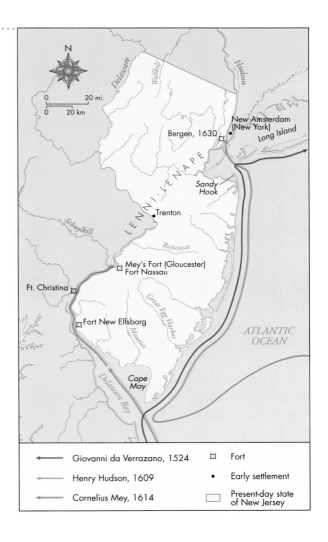

Exploration of New Jersey

Opposite: Henry Hudson descending what is now the Hudson River

Fur trading was big business between the Native Americans and the Dutch settlers.

Bergen, the First Settlement

The first permanent European settlement in New Jersey was a fort called *Bergen* (a Dutch word meaning "hill"), built in 1630. The log fort, about 800 square feet (74 sq m), was erected to fend off Indian attacks. Today Bergen Square, in the historic heart of Jersey City, stands on the site of that fort. Modern Bergen Square has a grim-faced statue of Peter Stuyvesant, the last Dutch governor of New Netherland. This governor was widely disliked for his harsh rule. ◼

Even before the Dutch established New Netherland, the British founded settlements in New England to the north and in Virginia to the south. Year by year, more English people arrived in these colonies. In 1664, British soldiers marched into New Netherland and won control of that region. Governor Peter Stuyvesant surrendered his principal city, New Amsterdam, without firing a shot. That city later became the gigantic metropolis of New York City.

King Charles II of England gave much of the former New Netherland to his brother James, Duke of York. The English then gave the northern region and its principal city the name that they have today—New York. James transferred the southern portion of the one-time Dutch land to two friends, John Berkeley and Sir George Carteret. Carteret had once served as governor of Jersey, an island in the English Channel. In honor of Carteret's service to the crown, the southern region was named New Jersey.

In the late 1600s, Quaker groups established the villages of Trenton and Mount Holly near the Delaware River. They were peace-loving people who got along well with their Indian neighbors. For a few decades, it seemed that New Jersey would become the home and religious retreat for many thousands of Quakers eager to leave England. However, the honor of a Quaker homeland went to Pennsylvania, New Jersey's neighbor to the west.

Sir George Carteret lands in New Jersey.

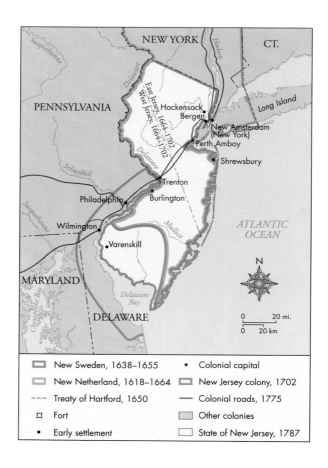

A Divided Colony

For the first four decades of its life, the British colony of New Jersey was divided into two halves—West Jersey and East Jersey. The division made it difficult for people to buy land. Complicating the situation, much of East Jersey was owned by a wealthy group of Quakers called the Twenty-four Proprietors. The Proprietors preferred to rent the land they owned rather than sell it. Finally, in 1702, England united the two Jerseys to form a single royal colony. Still, for more than seventy years, the colony of New Jersey had two capitals: Perth Amboy, the one-time capital of East Jersey, and Burlington, once the capital of West Jersey. ■

The principal leader of the English Quakers was the brilliant William Penn. In 1682, Penn tried to buy New Jersey land for the use of his followers. But land titles were so confused in divided New Jersey that Penn grew frustrated and asked the king for a title to what is now Pennsylvania. The title was granted and Penn founded Philadelphia on the west bank of the Delaware River. Under Penn's guidance, Philadelphia became as large as New York City. Thus New Jersey's fate was sealed very early in United States

history. Even then, it was the land that lay between New York City and Philadelphia.

The first Quaker meetinghouse, Burlington, New Jersey

Colonial Life

By 1726, the population of New Jersey had reached 32,422 people. In addition to English immigrants, the colony held large groups of Dutch, Swedes, and Germans. One out of twelve New Jersey residents at the time was African and the vast majority of blacks

**A nineteenth-century
New Jersey farmhouse**

were slaves. Some slaves were treated as members of the family by their masters, but in most cases a slave's life was horrible. In New Jersey, special courts judged slave lawbreakers. One law, written in 1695, said that a slave who stole a pig or a chicken "shall be publickly punished with corporal Punishment, not exceeding Forty Stripes [lashes with a whip]."

Under colonial laws, women had few rights. All property owned by a woman was automatically transferred to her husband when she married. One New Jersey law equated body decorations with witchcraft and forbade a woman from using "scents, cos-

Waterloo, a Restored Village

In the mid-1700s, Andover Forge was a prosperous northern New Jersey community. The town had a sawmill, an iron forge, and dozens of homes and churches. Much of that town is now preserved as Waterloo Village, which is near Stanhope. Visitors to Waterloo Village can watch craftspeople creating iron tools much as they did more than 200 years ago. ■

metics, washes, paints, artificial teeth, false hair, or high-heeled shoes."

Farms thrived on New Jersey's fertile soil. A Swedish traveler named Peter Kalm crossed New Jersey in the mid-1700s and saw corn "eight feet high, more or less." Kalm also marveled at New Jersey's peaches, a rare fruit in Europe. But in New Jersey, "every countryman had an orchard full of peach trees, which were covered with such quantities of fruit that we could scarcely walk without treading upon peaches that had fallen off." Kalm concluded that New Jersey residents conducted their lives "without any fear of poverty; for there is such a tract of good ground yet uncultivated."

Industries also blossomed in the colony. An ironworks operated at Shrewsbury, and the state's first glass-making factory was built at Allowaystown in 1740. Wagon roads, many of which followed old Lenni-Lenape footpaths, crisscrossed the colony. New Jersey had more miles of roadway than any of the other thirteen colonies. The first road linking Philadelphia with New York opened in 1764. At the time, a journey between the two cities took as long as four days. Travelers rode on "Jersey wagons," early versions of the covered wagon. These wagons, pulled by three to six horses, were developed in New Jersey in the 1730s.

Agriculture, industry, and trade spurred the growth of towns. Between 1710 and 1750, dozens of villages got their start: Orange, Freehold, New Brunswick, Princeton, Trenton, Newton, Hackensack, Morristown, Dover, Westfield, and Plainfield. Newark, which was destined to become the state's largest city, grew with the help of the leather industry.

The big losers in the development of colonial New Jersey were the Lenni-Lenape. After contact with the whites, the Native American people died in large numbers from smallpox and diphtheria,

The Elizabeth Town stagewagon (Jersey wagon), which advertised "Two days to Philadelphia"

New Jersey Pirates

Piracy was an enterprise that became New Jersey's shame. The many islands off New Jersey's coast were perfect hiding places for pirate ships to wait and then pounce upon merchant vessels. Notorious buccaneers such as Blackbeard (right) and Captain Kidd operated off Absecon Island near today's Atlantic City.

Legend says that Blackbeard buried a treasure chest in the Delaware River town of Burlington. The legend claims the chest was guarded by a Spaniard and his dog. More than 100 years later, Burlington residents insisted they saw the ghost of the dog prancing and growling in the night. ■

sicknesses against which they had no immunities. Alcoholism also took its toll. Many groups of Lenni-Lenape sold their land to whites and moved west. In 1758, a treaty established an Indian reservation at what is now the town of Indian Mills. By then, only about 200 members of the once-proud nation remained on New Jersey soil. Soon even those few disappeared. The Lenni-Lenape memory lingers, however, in New Jersey place names: Passaic, Totowa, Hopatcong, Kittatinny, Piscataway, Hoboken, and Ho-Ho-Kus.

Log-cabin schools, where they existed, served colonial New Jersey boys and girls. The schools were tiny and presided over by a single schoolmaster. Discipline was severe. A stick used to punish unruly students hung on the wall in full view of the class. Many children never attended school. Instead, these children were introduced to books at age thirteen or fourteen when they became apprentices. A New Jersey law stated that, in addition to a profes-

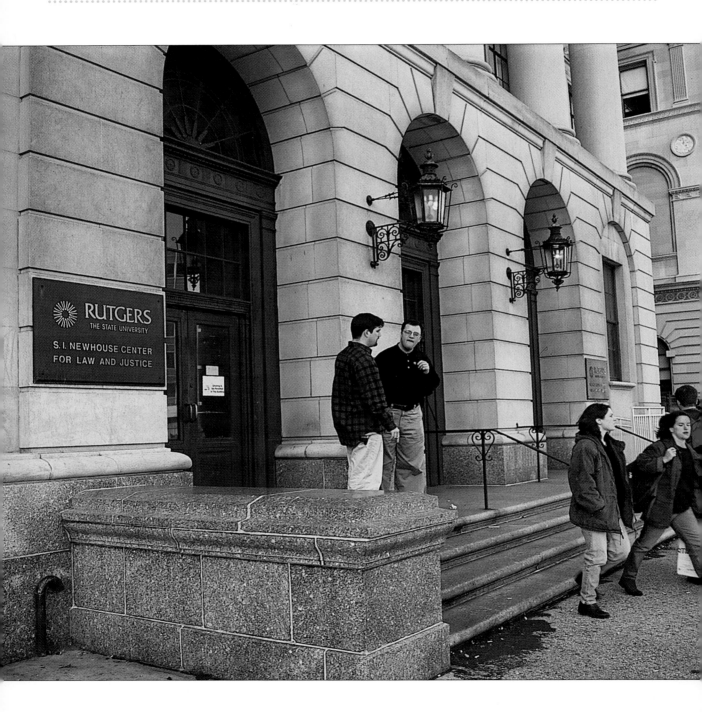

John Woolman, Philosopher of Colonial New Jersey

Education was promoted with zeal in Quaker communities, where people revered scholarship. Colonial New Jersey's leading Quaker was the Reverend John Woolman (1720–1772) of Mount Holly. He taught and wrote about many subjects, but his most passionate cause was the abolition of slavery. "I believe slave-keeping to be a practice inconsistent with the Christian religion," he declared from his pulpit. Often he journeyed to farms and implored owners to release their slaves. On rare occasions he convinced them. Woolman was one of the first Americans to raise his voice against the evils of slavery. ■

sion, all masters must teach their apprentices "to read, wryte, and cypher." During the colonial era, the College of New Jersey (later Princeton University) and Queen's College (later Rutgers University) were established. This made New Jersey the only British colony with more than one institution of higher learning.

By the 1770s, New Jersey's population stood at about 138,000. It was a prosperous colony, though overshadowed by its larger neighbors New York and Pennsylvania. At the time, the spirit of American independence stirred New Jersey and the other colonies. It was a spirit that would soon electrify the world.

Opposite: Present-day Rutgers University

CHAPTER THREE

Independence and Statehood

The Battle of Princeton

For 150 years, England lived at peace with its thirteen colonies on the shores of North America. Then, in 1763, after a long and costly conflict called the French and Indian War, Britain defeated France. That war drained the British Treasury, and Britain levied taxes on the American colonies to recoup its losses. Colonial resentment over the taxes led to war and finally to independence.

New Jersey and the American Revolution

The American Revolution was not a mass movement that saw the colonists rise up against Great Britain with one mind and one heart. Instead, many colonists chose to stay loyal to England, their mother country. The colony of New Jersey was about equally divided between men and women loyal to England and those who chose to rebel. One Loyalist was William Franklin, New Jersey's colonial governor. William was the son of Benjamin Franklin, the famous patriot. As governor, William Franklin urged New Jerseyites not to take up arms against the British. His father, on the other hand, was a leading figure advocating independence. After the war, father and son were never again on friendly terms.

Despite divisions among its people, New Jersey played a vital role in the American Revolution. In 1774, a group of New Jersey men, dressed as Indians, burned a shipload of British tea. The

Opposite: The Morris Canal

Molly Pitcher

A hero of the Battle of Monmouth was Mary Ludwig Hays, who was born in Trenton. On a steaming hot day in June 1778, Mary followed her husband, a gunner in the First Pennsylvania Artillery, into action. As the men fired the cannon, Molly served them pitchers of water. Finally her husband collapsed under the brutal sun. She took his place as a member of the crew, and the cannon continued lobbing shells at the British. Ever afterward, Mary Ludwig Hays was called "Molly Pitcher," and she became a legend. ∎

action, called the Greenwich Tea Burning, was taken in sympathy with the famous Boston Tea Party protest of 1773. During the war years, decisive battles took place in Trenton (1776), Princeton (1777), and Monmouth (1778). The commander of the American forces, George Washington, spent three winters in New Jersey.

One of the most famous engagements of the eight-year Revolutionary War was the 1776 Battle of Trenton. Washington chose the day after Christmas to assault Trenton, now New Jersey's capital city. General Washington hoped to surprise the Hessians (German mercenary soldiers serving in the British forces) who occupied the town. To approach Trenton, Washington and his troops had to cross the ice-choked Delaware River. The army then marched 9 miles (14 km) over pitch-dark roads through snow and sleet. The surprise attack worked to perfection. In a half-hour battle, Washington took 900 prisoners at the cost of just a few American casualties. One of Washington's men wounded at Trenton was Lieutenant James Monroe, who later became the fifth president of the United States.

"A Barrel Tapped at Both Ends"

The end of the Revolutionary War ushered in a period of expansion in New Jersey. Because of the state's position between New York City and Philadelphia, much energy was concentrated on improving its road system. Unfortunately, New Jersey's splendid progress in this area also cemented its image as being more a road than a state. Even the statesman Benjamin Franklin called New Jersey "a barrel tapped at both ends."

By 1830, fifty-four private turnpike companies operated in the state. The companies maintained roads and bridges and charged

An Artistic Legacy of Battle

The victory at Trenton uplifted the spirits of the colonial forces during a low point in the war. Later the battle was immortalized in "Washington Crossing the Delaware," an 1851 painting by the German-American artist Emanuel Leutze. The painting is inspirational but not correct in details. It shows Washington standing stiffly at the bow of his boat, something the general would never do. A standing man would have unbalanced the small boat and caused it to tip over into the icy Delaware River. ■

travelers a fee to use the roads. Those early turnpikes were crowded with horse-drawn carts, herders driving cows and sheep, and covered wagons taking pioneers to the West. Well-to-do travelers rode fast stagecoaches, which were sometimes called "flying wagons," but even the fastest coaches took a day to get from New York to Philadelphia over the rough and rocky roads. And the journey was miserable, causing many passengers to become nauseated. One traveler found the turnpike near New Brunswick "full of loose stones and deep holes, in going over which we were so vio-

New Jersey roads were first used only for a few stagecoaches and farm carts. But as the state grew, the roads had to improve.

Opposite: *The Johnny Bull,* a locomotive that ran between Camden and Perth Amboy

lently shook, that when we got down, many of us could scarcely stand."

A bold industrial project was launched at Paterson, site of a mighty 77-foot (23.5 m) waterfall. For years, the waterfall on the Passaic River had been a tourist attraction. During the Revolutionary War, George Washington and his associate Alexander Hamilton had lunch at the foot of the great falls. Hamilton, always a visionary, saw the waterfall's potential for driving water-

The Burr–Hamilton Duel

Alexander Hamilton, the country's first secretary of state, was a brilliant but stubborn politician who made many enemies in government. One of his bitterest enemies was Aaron Burr, then vice president of the United States. In 1804, Burr challenged Hamilton to meet him on the dueling grounds at Weehawken, New Jersey. There, over-looking the Hudson River, the two faced each other with pistols in their hands. Burr shot Hamilton, and Hamilton died a few hours later. Burr had to flee the state because New Jersey law forbade dueling. The duel at Weehawken was the most famous of its kind in U.S. history. It cost Hamilton his life and ruined Burr's political career. ■

wheels and providing power to factories. In the 1790s, Hamilton laid out a town at the waterfall and encouraged industries to build there. The town was called Paterson in honor of New Jersey's governor, William Paterson. One of the early factories in Paterson was owned by the firearms manufacturer Samuel Colt. The deadly Colt .45, the "gun that made the West," was manufactured in Paterson.

In the late 1820s, New Jersey began a busy period of canal building. The Morris Canal ran from Newark to Phillipsburg, and the Delaware and Raritan Canal linked New Brunswick to Bordentown. Both canals crossed the state, allowing canal boats to go from the Delaware River to the Atlantic shore. Canal boats were flat-bottomed barges drawn over the canal's waters by horses or mules. The animals walked along a towpath beside the canal. Usually the boats carried bulk cargo such as coal or gravel. The 90-mile (145-km) Morris Canal was hailed as one of the engineering marvels of the nineteenth century. The Delaware and Raritan Canal remained in use until the 1930s. But both canals were soon overshadowed by a new and more exciting form of transport—railroads.

New Jersey's first railroad began operations in 1834 between the cities of Camden and Perth Amboy. The railroad was operated by Robert L. Stevens, the son of inventor John Stevens. It was an innovative railroad line—its trains ran on iron rails instead of the wooden rails used elsewhere. Robert Stevens developed the "hook-headed" spike still used today to

New Jersey Becomes a State

The Revolutionary War officially ended in 1783 when a treaty granted the thirteen colonies independence. Seven years earlier, on July 2, 1776, New Jersey adopted its own constitution and declared itself a state. Thus New Jersey proclaimed statehood two days before the other colonies made that bold move. The town of Trenton became the official state capital in 1790. ■

John Stevens, New Jersey Inventor

John Stevens (1749–1838) lived in Perth Amboy and in Hoboken. A mechanical genius, he often tinkered with the newly developed concept of steam-powered engines. In 1804, he built a steam-powered ship that crossed the Hudson River. Stevens accomplished this feat three years before Robert Fulton's famous steamboat, the *Clermont*, took to the waters. Stevens next built the first successful steam locomotive in the United States. He operated the locomotive on a circular track on his farm in Hoboken. The engine, called a "steam wagon," reached a speed of 12 miles (19.3 km) per hour.

fasten rails onto wooden cross ties. On the railroad's initial run, the locomotive struck a stray hog and skipped off the track. A witness claimed a passenger "in his fright turned a somersault out the window." Despite the mishap, the railroad expanded and built the first line from New York City to Philadelphia in 1840. Trains by that time were able to reach the breakneck speed of 30 miles (48 km) an hour.

Brother against Brother

Hampering progress in both New Jersey and the United States was the daunting issue of slavery. By the 1850s, the nation was being torn asunder by the slavery question. Explosive arguments over slavery led to the bloodiest war in the nation's history—a war that pitted brother against brother.

It was not until 1804 that New Jersey passed laws granting gradual freedom to the state's slaves, becoming the last state in the Northeast to pass such laws. New Jersey had more slaves than any other state in the North, and many white residents were staunch supporters of slavery. About 25 percent of New Jersey's soil lay below the Mason-Dixon Line, the widely recognized border between the North and the South.

Even though the state had many Southern sympathizers, hundreds of New Jerseyites risked their lives by joining a secret organization called the Underground Railroad. This organization was a network of households devoted to the aid of escaping slaves. Its members opened their houses to runaways, fed them, and told them where they could find the next "safe house" on the Underground Railroad. New Jersey's Underground Railroad was led by Quakers. Many escaped slaves settled in the community of Lawnside, near Camden, and their descendants live there to this day.

New Jersey contributed 88,000 troops to the Northern forces during the Civil War (1861–1865). More than 6,000 New Jersey men died during the fighting. New Jersey units sometimes marched into battle singing their special song:

The brave volunteers of New Jersey,
All patriots, noble and true;
Aroused at the call of our country,
We'll stand by the red, white, and blue.

The Trusts Take Power

After the Civil War, industry expanded rapidly—too rapidly, according to some critics. Corporations began to control state government. With millionaire business owners handing money to politicians, New Jersey wrote tax laws that were favorable to big

Industrialist John D. Rockefeller moved his Standard Oil Company to New Jersey.

business. Low taxes encouraged tycoon John D. Rockefeller, then the world's richest man, to move his Standard Oil Company to New Jersey. Bayonne became a major oil-refining center when Standard Oil built a plant there. Large corporations such as Standard Oil were called "trusts." Outraged citizens claimed New Jersey was "the mother of the trusts."

New Jersey industries grew at a time when European immigrants were flowing into the United States. The immigrants were processed in offices at Ellis Island, a rocky outcropping off the New Jersey shore. Most of the newcomers came from southern and eastern Europe, and thousands took factory jobs in Newark, Elizabeth, and Paterson. The city of Passaic had the highest proportion of foreign-born residents in the United States, according to the 1910 census. By 1930, Italians were the state's largest ethnic group, followed by Germans, Poles, Irish, and Russians. The former Protestant Dutch and English state was now home to Roman Catholics and Eastern European Jews. The Ellis Island generation changed the face of New Jersey forever.

The Wizard of Menlo Park

The 131-foot (40-m) Edison Memorial Tower stands in Menlo Park topped by a glowing 14-foot (4-m) lightbulb. In 1876, Thomas Edison opened a laboratory in Menlo Park and concentrated on creating inventions that he said would meet "the desperate needs of the world." During the next ten years, he improved upon the telephone and the typewriter and invented the phonograph and the electric lightbulb. Of the 1,093 inventions Edison patented, more than 400 were developed at Menlo Park. A replica of his first laboratory now stands near the tower. Inside are photographs and models of the items created by this New Jersey genius—the Wizard of Menlo Park. ■

Immigrants arrive at
Ellis Island in 1915.

Who Owns Ellis Island?

Ellis Island operated as an immigration processing center from 1892 through 1954. It was the gateway for more than 12 million newcomers to this country. Ellis Island is now a museum that is visited by thousands of people each day. For decades, the island was considered to be a part of New York State, even though it lay closer to New Jersey. In 1997, New York and New Jersey submitted a plan to the U.S. Supreme Court to divide ownership of the island. The federal government actually owns the island, however, because it is a national park. ■

CHAPTER FOUR

The Modern State

Downtown Newark, 1935

n the twentieth century, New Jersey saw the rise and decline of industry, and its cities fought the influx of crime and drugs. But New Jersey's problems were no greater than those faced by any other industrialized state. Many people from neighboring areas moved to the Garden State. Finally, New Jersey, the place that was betwixt and between, assumed its proper position as one of America's great states.

Reform

In the early 1900s, corporations had so thoroughly taken over the government that writer Lincoln Steffens called New Jersey the "traitor state." Laws passed by the New Jersey legislature favored business owners over workers. As a result, working men and

Opposite: Port Newark

SENSATIONAL AND STARTLING "HOLD UP" OF THE "GOLD EXPRESS," BY FAMOUS WESTERN OUTLAWS

The Silver Screen

One New Jersey industry—the movies—brought glamour to the state. In 1889, the New Jersey-based genius Thomas Edison perfected the kinetoscope, a practical motion-picture projector. The first successful commercial film, *The Great Train Robbery,* was shot in New Jersey in 1903. A movie industry blossomed in the town of Fort Lee. Silent-screen idols such as Mary Pickford, Pearl White, and Roscoe "Fatty" Arbuckle worked at New Jersey studios. But soon the movie companies moved their capital to a sunnier spot— a tiny California town named Hollywood. ■

women were unprotected, and the deplorable practice of child labor became widespread.

Near the turn of the century, a state inspector examined New Jersey factories and was appalled by the number of small children he saw working there: "The average age at which these children went to work was nine years. . . . All of them worked ten hours a day and many of them thirteen or more." Factory jobs, of course, kept the children from attending school. The inspector continued his report: "There is no exaggeration in saying that three-fourths of the working children know absolutely nothing. . . . Very few of these children, the large majority of whom were born in the United States, ever heard of George Washington. . . . Many big girls and boys were unable to say whether New Jersey was in North or South America."

In 1910, the people of New Jersey elected Woodrow Wilson as their governor. A college professor and former president of Princeton University, he brought fresh ideas to government. Wilson, who was born in Virginia, sponsored laws that made state elections more democratic. He also forced businesses to pay for workers' injuries and punished corrupt politicians. Wilson's bold work in reforming New Jersey government brought him national attention. In 1912, Woodrow Wilson was elected the twenty-eighth president of the United States.

Despite the efforts of Wilson and other reformers, however, corrupt politicians remained in power in New Jersey. Most notorious of the political bosses was Frank "I am the Law" Hague. First elected mayor of Jersey City in 1917, Hague got his nickname because he was indeed the law—and some say the only law—in Hudson County. Hague relied on immigrant voters to march to the polls on Election Day. The voters were rewarded with Christmas food baskets and summertime picnics. Hague controlled county and state jobs and ran the Jersey City police force as if it were his private army. He also amassed money. Hague never earned more than $7,500 a year as mayor of Jersey City, yet he somehow acquired a fortune of $8 million. At his funeral in 1956, an elderly

Woodrow Wilson was New Jersey's governor before becoming president of the United States.

Frank "I am the Law" Hague

woman from Jersey City carried a sign that read, "God have mercy on his sinful, greedy soul."

New Jersey in Peace and War

In 1917, the United States entered World War I (1914–1918). Almost 73,000 young New Jerseyites served in the conflict. Men and women from all over the country trained at Camp Merritt near Cresskill and at Camp Dix in the forests of Burlington County. By war's end, New Jersey had sixteen military-training facilities. The state's industries churned out war materials at an astonishing rate. Huge shipyards at Newark, Camden, and Kearny made New Jersey the country's leading shipbuilder. New Jersey munitions plants produced millions of artillery shells and ships left the docks at Hoboken each day taking supplies and soldiers to the fighting fronts of Europe. Tens of thousands of Americans died in World War I. For most, Hoboken was their last glimpse of home.

By 1930, New Jersey's population had swelled to 4 million, making it the ninth most populous state in the nation. Just forty years earlier, it ranked eighteenth. Towns clustered in the north near New York marked the beginnings of the state's suburban growth. In 1930, the five counties near New York City held 2.5 million people, 75 percent of the state's population.

During the 1930s, New Jersey and the United States fell into the grips of the Great Depression. Nationally, one of every four workers was unemployed. By 1936, more than 700,000 New Jersey men and women were collecting some form of welfare and workers who had kept their jobs lived in fear of a layoff. Signs over factory doors read: NO HELP WANTED.

The Game That Immortalized Atlantic City

During the Great Depression, families entertained themselves at home because they could not afford movie tickets. With this thought in mind, an out-of-work salesman named Charles Darrow dreamed up the board game Monopoly in 1933. Darrow named properties such as Park Place and Ventnor Avenue after streets in his favorite vacation spot: Atlantic City, New Jersey. Shortly after its introduction, Monopoly was America's favorite game. When Atlantic City leaders attempted to rename Baltic and Mediterranean Avenues in 1973, Monopoly-lovers shouted out their anger. The city dropped its plans, and one city leader penned a poem:

To this ordinance vote no.
To our residents it presents a great
woe.
Baltic and Mediterranean are
streets we know.
Without them we could never pass
GO. ■

The Depression proved difficult for all of New Jersey. However, according to Giles R. Wright in *Afro-Americans in New Jersey*, African-Americans in particular were strongly affected:

Of all the New Jersey ethnic groups, Afro-Americans suffered most during the Depression of the 1930s. In 1932 black unemployment in the state was nearly twice that of whites. And once blacks lost their jobs they tended to remain unemployed longer than whites.

Japanese bombs fell on Pearl Harbor, Hawaii, on December 7, 1941. Americans were shocked, frightened, and outraged. The Great Depression ended in a flurry of wartime industrial production. Once more, ships were assembled with furious speed in yards

John Basilone, New Jersey Hero

The 1943 invasion of Guadalcanal was one of the toughest battles the U.S. Marine Corps ever fought. John Basilone, a machine gunner from the town of Raritan, defended his position even when surrounded by attacking Japanese. His machine gun overheated and broke down, but Basilone held off the enemy with his pistol. For his heroic actions on Guadalcanal, he was awarded the Congressional Medal of Honor. Afterward he was ordered to the United States where he participated in parades designed to sell war bonds. Basilone, the son of Italian immigrants, did not enjoy his sudden fame and asked to return to combat. He was killed during the 1945 Marine assault on Iwo Jima. Basilone's statue now stands in Raritan, where an annual parade is held in his honor.

at Newark and Camden. The state's diversified factories produced radios, uniforms, airplane engines, and countless other war necessities. One Hoboken company even raised spiders for the war effort. Tiny strands of the spiders' webs were used as crosshairs in telescopes and bombsights. More than 500,000 New Jersey men and women served in the armed forces. Seventeen New Jerseyites won the Congressional Medal of Honor, the nation's highest award for bravery.

New Jersey contributed directly to the end of World War II and the beginning of the nuclear age. In 1939, Albert Einstein wrote a letter to President Franklin Roosevelt warning him that Nazi Germany had the capacity to build an atomic bomb. Einstein was a professor at Princeton and a world-renowned expert on nuclear theory. After reading the letter, Roosevelt ordered research to begin and eventually launched a nuclear-bomb program. Einstein

Albert Einstein

was a gentle genius who lived quietly at 112 Mercer Street in Princeton. Though he hated war, his letter to the president led to the birth of the most destructive weapon ever created.

Modern New Jersey

The postwar era saw a sea of suburbs spread over what was once farmland and pastures. The building boom was especially prominent in the northeast, where cities such as Middleton Township, Woodbridge, and Clifton tripled in population. This stunning growth was fueled by the automobile. After the war, everyone wanted a family car.

Construction of the New Jersey Turnpike began in 1950.

New Jersey, being a crossroads state, became a national leader in highway building. Construction of the 134-mile (216-km) New Jersey Turnpike began in 1950 and was completed two years later. Running between New York City and Philadelphia, the turnpike became the nation's busiest superhighway—and one of the safest. The New Jersey Turnpike was the first major highway to install guardrails along its entire length. The rails prevented out-of-control vehicles from crossing the median strip and causing head-on collisions. Similar guardrails were soon adopted by other states, where they were called "Jersey Rails." The Garden State Parkway opened in 1954 and takes motorists through some

The Garden State Parkway opened in 1954.

The New Jersey Turnpike Hall of Fame

Service areas on the New Jersey Turnpike are named for famous people who either were born or lived in the state. The Clara Barton Service Area is named after the founder of the American Red Cross (right), who taught school in Bordentown. The Grover Cleveland Service Area is named for the United States president (first elected in 1884), born in Caldwell.

The James Fenimore Cooper Service Area honors the novelist, author of *The Last of the Mohicans,* who grew up on a farm in Burlington County. The William Halsey Service Area is named for the famous World War II naval commander, born in Elizabeth. The Molly Pitcher Service Area celebrates the Revolutionary War heroine. ■

of New Jersey's finest scenery. Other major highways completed in the post–World War II era include the Atlantic City Expressway and the Palisades Interstate Parkway.

Suburban New Jersey promised the good life for those who had moved out of overcrowded New York City. Suburbs also developed outside of New Jersey's aging industrial centers such as Newark and Paterson. But during the suburbanization process, the old inner cities deteriorated.

Into the cities moved African-Americans from the South. Many blacks were lured north by wartime industrial jobs. Unlike the immigrants who came to the state during the Ellis Island years, the newly arriving African-Americans faced housing discrimination. They had no choice but to live in the big city housing projects. Newark, Camden, East Orange, and Plainfield developed an African-American majority population. Shortly after the influx, the outmoded city factories began closing in favor of new facilities built in the suburbs. The situation left the inner cities crowded with people and short of jobs.

When racial unrest and the gloom of the Vietnam War gripped the country in the late 1960s, much of urban New Jersey was tense. Experts warned of an explosion. The city of Newark seemed most volatile. Newark had twice as much unemployment as the rest of the nation, and its slums were notorious for filth and neglect. No other city in the United States had more condemned buildings.

On July 12, 1967, an African-American cabdriver was arrested by Newark police for a traffic violation. The driver fought with the officers. Rumors spread through Newark's Central Ward that the driver had been beaten to death. Mobs took to the streets, looting

Opposite: The National Guard on the streets of Newark during the 1967 riots

New Jersey's Scientific Firsts

Scientific research leading to inventions and new products has a long history in New Jersey. Here are a few state "firsts":

In 1837, Samuel F. B. Morse developed the first electrical telegraph in a shop in Morristown.

In the late 1800s, while living in New Jersey, Thomas Edison invented the first lightbulb, movie projector, and camera, as well as a workable typewriter.

John P. Holland (right) built the world's first successful submarine in 1878 and operated it on the Passaic River; the submarine, called *Fenian Ram,* is now displayed at a Paterson museum.

In 1882, Roselle became the world's first city to be fully illuminated by electric streetlights.

The first electric sewing machine was developed in 1889 by the Singer Company in Elizabeth.

Lee De Forest of Jersey City built the first vacuum tube in 1907; the tube made modern radio and TV possible.

The air conditioner was invented in 1911 by Willis Carrier, who worked out of his factory in Newark.

The transistor was developed in 1947 by a team at Bell Laboratories in Murray Hill. In 1951, Bell engineers in Englewood created the equipment that made the first direct-dial long-distance telephone call to California. Prior to this time, all long-distance calls had to be made through an operator.

Bell scientists from New Jersey also designed Telstar, a communications satellite launched in 1962 that transmitted the first live television programs across the Atlantic. ▨

stores and burning buildings, and gunfights broke out between police and rioters. Said one Newark resident, "I thought this must be like war is, to be in the middle of it." The rioting lasted five days, twenty-seven people were killed, and property damage was estimated at $10 million. The Newark riot was one of the worst in American history.

Suburbanization continued long after the fires of Newark died. Strip malls opened just outside the state's many historic towns. For generations, stores and offices in those towns had been located on the central avenue, often called Main Street. Then came the strip malls offering plenty of parking. Customers flocked to the malls, leaving boarded-up storefronts on Main Streets. The popular songwriter Bruce Springsteen, who grew up in Freehold and got his start as a singer in Asbury Park, lamented this development in his song "My Hometown," which is about the demise of Main Street.

New Jersey's economic picture brightened in the 1980s and 1990s as the state became a center for scientific research. No other state of comparable size had more working scientists. Pharmaceutical firms such as the huge Hoffman-La Roche Company near Clifton developed drugs to fight illness. In the 1980s, AT&T, the giant telephone company, became New Jersey's biggest non-government employer. However, most of the research jobs were open to educated workers only. Those without an education or a technical skill were left behind in the job market.

Finally, and perhaps most important, New Jersey began to lose its frustrating image. No longer was the state regarded as a colony for its larger neighbors. The 1990 census counted 7.7 million people living in New Jersey as opposed to 7.3 million in New York

New Jersey singer
and storyteller Bruce
Springsteen

City. This marked the first time in 150 years that Garden State residents outnumbered people living in the urban giant to the north. New Jersey's main growth areas in the 1990s were in the central parts of the state, away from its "big brothers." The Garden State also generated more new jobs in the 1990s than did New York or Pennsylvania. New residents, attracted by these jobs, identified with New Jersey. It was their state. And few people told "Jersey jokes" anymore.

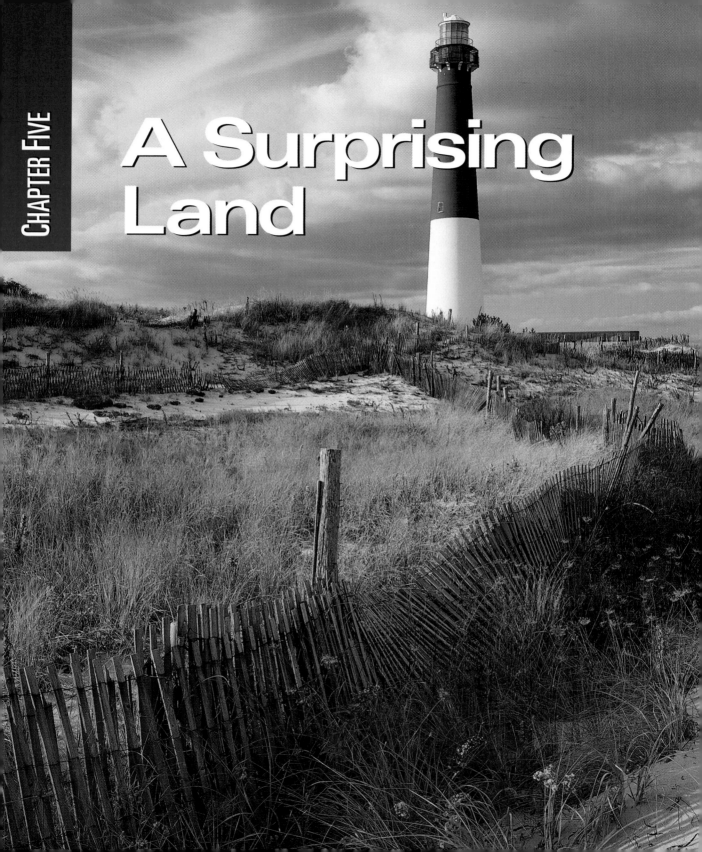

CHAPTER FIVE

A Surprising Land

Cherry trees in Belleville

From its lake country to its shoreline to its farmland, the Garden State surprises visitors. Many first-time travelers exclaim breathlessly, "I had no idea New Jersey was so beautiful." The surprises await people who explore nature's marvels in state parks and forests and those who take the time to smell the flowers along the way.

Land Forms

New Jersey is small, forty-sixth in size among the fifty states. To the west, the Delaware River forms the state's border with Pennsylvania. In the north and northeast, the state line and the Hudson River mark the border with New York State. In the east is the Atlantic Ocean. New Jersey is one of the three Middle Atlantic states, along with New York and Pennsylvania.

Opposite: The Jersey Shore and Barnegat Lighthouse

The Delaware Water Gap, one of the most amazing sights in New Jersey

Geologists divide New Jersey into four major land regions: (1) the Appalachian Ridge cuts across the state's northwest corner and contains the lesser mountains of the great Appalachian mountain chain; (2) the New England Uplands, also called the highlands, holds many of the state's lovely lakes; (3) the Piedmont is an area of rolling hills in which New Jersey's largest cities are located; and (4) the Atlantic Coastal Plain is a moist, fairly level region that covers the southern two-thirds of the state.

A highlight of the Appalachian Ridge region is the Delaware Water Gap in the northwest corner of New Jersey, one of the biggest surprises in the Surprising State. Travelers heading east from Pennsylvania on Route 80 are suddenly confronted with a marvelous canyon carved out of mountains by the Delaware River. The rugged gorge stuns those seeing it for the first time. Visitors climb foot trails up Mount Tammany, which overlooks the river. Tammany is part of a mountain range called the Kittatinnies—"big mountains" in a Native American language. Certainly the climb is exhausting, but the view from the top is worth every step.

New Jersey's Geographical Features

Total area; rank	8,215 sq. mi. (21,277 sq km); 46th
Land; rank	7,419 sq. mi. (19,215 sq km); 46th
Water; rank	796 sq. mi. (2,062 sq km); 33rd
Inland water; rank	371 sq. mi. (961 sq km); 39th
Coastal water; rank	425 sq. mi. (1,101 sq km); 13th
Geographic center	Mercer, 5 miles (8 km) southeast of Trenton
Highest point	High Point, 1,803 feet (550 m)
Lowest point	Sea level along Atlantic Ocean
Largest city	Newark
Longest river	Raritan River, 75 miles (121 km)
Population; rank	7,748,634 (1990); 9th
Record high temperature	110°F (43°C) at Runyon on July 10, 1936
Record low temperature	−34°F (−37°C) at River Vale on January 5, 1904
Average July temperature	75°F (24°C)
Average January temperature	31°F (−1°C)
Average annual precipitation	45 inches (114 cm)

High Point State Park

High Point State Park in the Kittatinny Mountains lies near the town of Montague. One mountain peak at High Point stands 1,803 feet (550 m) above sea level, making it the highest point in New Jersey. The land was donated to the state by the Kuser family, avid bird-watchers who wanted to establish a nature sanctuary.

High Point State Park is laced with hiking trails. Altogether, New Jersey has more than 4,000 miles (6,452 km) of hiking trails. Strung together, they would stretch the length of the United States. ■

Sparkling lakes abound in the New England Uplands. These lakes were created by glaciers that crawled over the land 10,000 to 20,000 years ago. The largest lake in the region—and New Jersey's biggest—is Lake Hopatcong, roughly 6 miles (10 km) long and 2 miles (3.2 km) wide. Its name comes from a Lenni-Lenape word meaning "honey water of many coves." Hopatcong has been altered over the years by canals and dams. The lake provides a popular recreation area for northern New Jersey city dwellers. On a busy day, more than 6,000 motorboats, sailboats, and canoes bob on Hopatcong's waters.

Opposite, top: Lake Hopatcong got its name from the Lenni-Lenape word for "honey water of many coves."

Several of the state's major rivers wind through the Piedmont region. These rivers include the Passaic, the Ramapo, and the Raritan. The 75-mile (121-km) Raritan River is the longest river lying wholly within New Jersey. Also in the Piedmont area is the broad Hudson River, which marks New Jersey's border with New York State.

In the south, the Atlantic Coastal Plain has two prominent features—the Atlantic Ocean Shore and the Pine Barrens. In New Jersey, the Atlantic coast is always called the Jersey Shore or simply the Shore. The Jersey Shore, which runs nearly 130 miles (210 km) along the Atlantic, is one of the great coastal playgrounds in the United States. Tourists flock there to enjoy the sandy beaches, explore long narrow islands, and visit resort towns such as Atlantic City, Ocean Grove, Wildwood, and Asbury Park.

The New Jersey Shore is lined with long and narrow islands called barrier islands. These islands were formed over thousands of years by rivers washing sand and silt into the ocean. Waves then molded the sands into long finger-shaped islands that run parallel to the coastline. Much of the United States eastern shore is laced with barrier islands. One

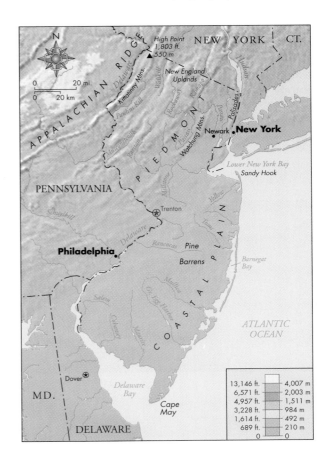

New Jersey's topography

Sandy Hook, on the tip
of a barrier island

prominent barrier island in New Jersey is Absecon, home to Atlantic City.

The Pine Barrens, also called the Pinelands, covers 1,000 square miles (2,590 sq km) and touches on seven counties. This vast pine forest is laced by a few gravel roads and little more. While New Jersey as a whole has 995 people per square mile (2.59 sq km) the Pine Barrens has a mere 15 people for every square mile. The soil of the Pine Barrens often feels moist to the touch because underneath the woodlands lies a vast reservoir containing some 7 trillion gallons (27 trillion l) of fresh water. It is the largest freshwater reserve on the eastern seaboard of the United States.

Island Beach State Park, a Jersey Shore Getaway Spot

Near the town of Toms River, this 1,900-acre (770 ha) park stands on one of the last relatively undisturbed barrier islands on the East Coast. At the park's beach, which is about 1 mile (1.6 km) long, visitors swim in the ocean and fish from the shore. Miles of hiking trails wind around the sand dunes. ■

The New Jersey Devil

The Pine Barrens is the source of New Jersey's most famous legend. The story goes that in the early 1800s, a Pine Barrens woman was pregnant with what would be her thirteenth child. "I would rather have a devil than another baby," the angry woman proclaimed. She got her wish. The baby was born with the face of a horse and the wings of a bat. It flew out of the mother's house and into a nearby swamp. There, as the devil, it tormented Pine Barrens people for years to come. Today, the New Jersey Devil is looked upon in a more playful light. Schoolchildren are told the story and asked to draw pictures of the devil. Prizes are offered to the most imaginative young artists. ▪

White-tailed deer live throughout New Jersey's forests.

Nature and Climate

Cape May Point State Park lies on the southern tip of New Jersey. The plants and shrubs there are among the most diverse in the world. Growing on park grounds are shrubs such as Japanese honeysuckle and southern arrowhead. Trees include sweet bay magnolia and bigtooth aspen. In all, more than 300 species of plants thrive in the 190-acre (77-ha) park. Cape May Point State Park is also a stopping-off place for migratory hawks. Nearby, the Cape May Migratory Bird Refuge provides a protected nesting area for many birds, including endangered species such as the peregrine falcon and the upland sandpiper.

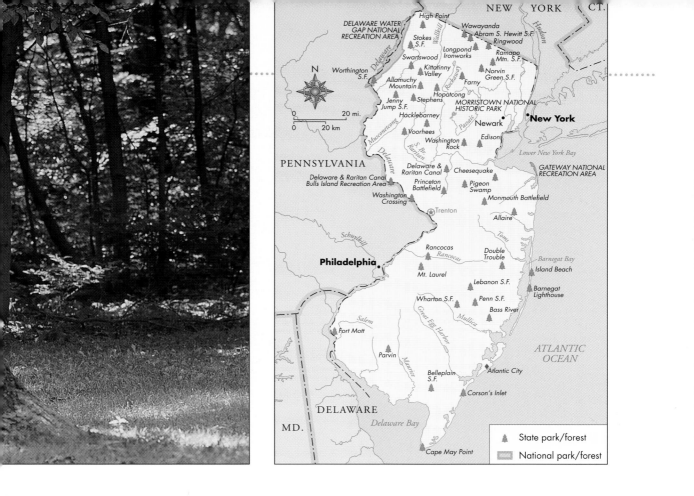

The Bass River State Park is located near the town of New Gretna. A 23,257-acre (9,416-ha) nature reserve, the park protects a rare pine species. Guests take a self-guided nature trail through stands of pine, oak, and white cedar bog. The park sits on transitional land, where softwood and hardwood trees merge. Orchids and sparkling jewelweed grow along its trails, and squirrels, chipmunks, and raccoons scurry across the forest floor. Bass swim in the waters of Bass River State Park, along with pickerel, sunfish, and catfish.

New Jersey is known for its industries, its crowded cities, and its seemingly endless suburbs. Less known is the fact that

New Jersey's parks and forests

The Palisades

Another New Jersey natural wonder is a breathtaking series of cliffs called The Palisades. Running 15 miles (24 km) along the western side of the Hudson River, the cliffs stand 500 feet (152 m) tall. The best view of these magnificent cliffs is from Palisades Interstate Park at Fort Lee. The Henry Hudson Drive in Fort Lee, which is closed to cars during the summer months, allows people to cycle and jog along the cliffside. ■

40 percent of New Jersey is forested and that it has more than 800 lakes and ponds. The Garden State maintains fifty wildlife-management areas and more than 150,000 acres (60,703 ha) of state game preserves. Deer, black bear, foxes, opossums, rabbits, and skunks roam in the wilderness regions. In recent years, coyote and beaver have returned. Marshlands are home to wild ducks and geese, while pheasants, quail, and wild turkeys inhabit the meadows. Bass, bluefish, crappies, pike, and trout splash in the streams, while the Jersey Shore teems with a wide variety of fish, as well as clams, crabs, lobsters, and oysters.

New Jersey meadows provide homes for pheasants and other birds.

New Jersey's climate is typical of the Middle Atlantic states. Summers are warm and humid, but they are made more pleasant by ocean breezes that blow inland from the shore. Average July temperatures range from 70° to 76° F (21° to 24° C). Rainfall is ample and evenly distributed throughout the state. In winter, northern New Jersey gets about 50 inches (127 cm) of snow, while the south averages only about 13 inches (33 cm). January temperatures average 34° F (1° C) in the south and 26° F (−3° C) in the Appalachian Ridge region to the north.

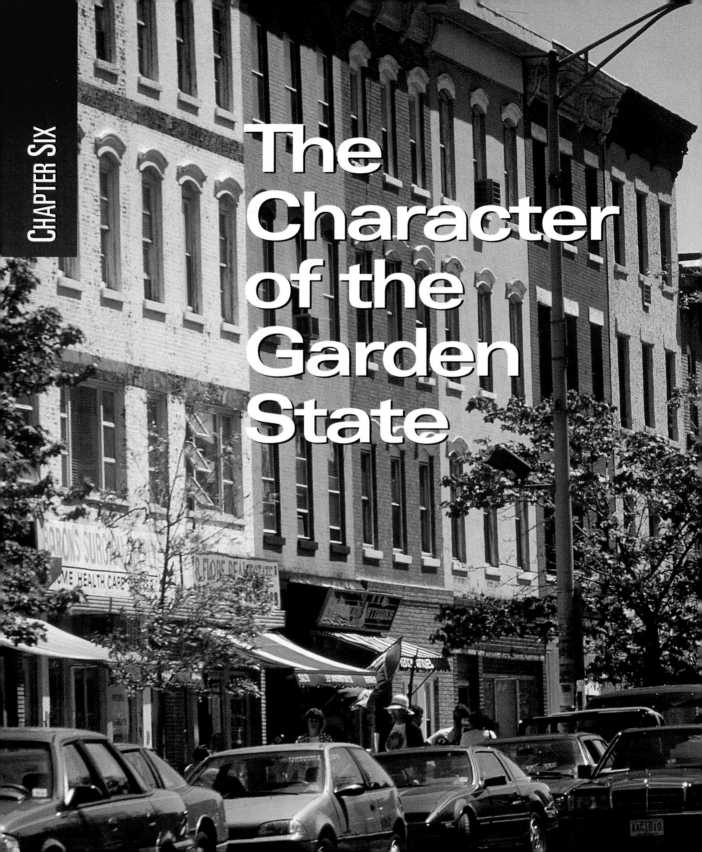

CHAPTER SIX

The Character of the Garden State

**N**ine of every ten New Jerseyites live in cities or towns. For more than 100 years, the majority of the state's residents have been city folks. This long-term attachment to cities has given New Jersey a unique blend of historic towns and modern suburbs.

Washington Park in Newark

The Northeast

Northeastern New Jersey is a belt of cities that cluster near New York City, the giant across the Hudson. More than two-thirds of New Jersey's population live in the old cities full of historic landmarks as well as in the suburbs that sprouted up after World War II.

Hoboken sits almost in the shadows of New York City's tallest buildings. For years, it was thought of as a tough seaport, infamous for its tavern brawls. Today Hoboken—the name comes from a Lenni-Lenape word meaning "land of the tobacco pipe"—is a developing town with trendy restaurants and shops. New York City stockbrokers and bankers have bought houses here. Especially coveted are Hoboken's famous row houses, some of which are 150 years old. Rooms inside the row houses are only about 20 feet (6 m) wide, but the houses are four stories high. Wealthy people who moved into Hoboken's inner city spent thousands of dollars refurbishing these unusual houses.

Opposite: A typical Hoboken street

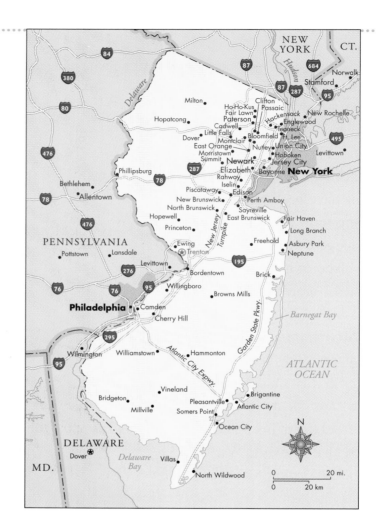

New Jersey's cities and interstates

From Swamp to Promised Land

For generations, the Meadowlands was a large and rather forbidding marshland that spread over the New Jersey side of the Hudson River. The 18,000-acre (7,287-ha) swamp lies almost in the shadows of New York City's skyscrapers. In the early 1970s, parts of the Meadowlands were drained, and Giants Stadium, used for football and soccer, was built. A sports center and more than 100 office and warehouse buildings soon followed. The one-time eyesore became one of the most valuable pieces of land in the world. ■

Factories stand empty in the once-industrial city of Paterson, but the great waterfall and other attractions remain. The falls are 77 feet (23.5 m) high, and as wide as a football field is long. Nearby is Lambert Castle, built in 1892 by Catholina Lambert, a British immigrant who once worked in a textile factory for thirty cents a week. Lambert made his fortune in Paterson. Today, visitors come from around the country to tour what used to be his house and view his private collection of artwork.

Lambert Castle, built in 1892

A Movie Image of Hoboken

The 1954 movie *On the Waterfront* was set in Hoboken. The film starred Marlon Brando as a laborer and former boxer who battled corrupt union bosses. *On the Waterfront* was a powerful movie, but it cemented Hoboken's image as a bruising, dangerous town. Only now is that image fading. ■

Hackensack is the brunt of jokes linking it to greasy restaurants and low-class bowling alleys. The jokes are unfair because Hackensack is an interesting and historic town. Its name derives from a minor Native American tribe called the Achkinkehacky. Early settlers could not pronounce this tongue twister, and the name Hackensack was soon in general use. Its courthouse, built in 1912, is an architectural gem. Downtown stands the First Reformed Church, erected in 1791. Hundreds of World War II buffs come to Hackensack to visit the USS *Ling,* a submarine commissioned in 1945 and now displayed in a museum.

Jersey City is New Jersey's second-largest city. It grew as a transportation and industrial center. Its industries declined shortly after World War II, but—like Hoboken—Jersey City is now a rediscovered metropolis. Jersey City is the entrance (or the exit) to the Holland Tunnel. The tunnel, opened in 1927, runs under the

USS *Ling*, a submarine that is part of a Hackensack museum

Hudson River and into the heart of New York City. Business owners and professionals who work in New York have restored Jersey City's handsome old brownstone houses. Lincoln Park, Jersey City's most popular playground, fills with more than 30,000 people on summer weekends.

Montclair is one of the prettiest towns in all New Jersey. Throughout the city stand 100-year-old mansions built by the wealthy merchants of New York City, and many are still owned by descendants of the original builders. Nearby towns such as Bloomfield, Nutley, Little Falls, Caldwell, and Clifton have seen their tra-

Newport Marina at Jersey City

Birthplace of Grover Cleveland

Only one American president was born on New Jersey soil—Grover Cleveland, born in Caldwell in 1837. Cleveland was elected president in 1884 and again in 1892. His birthplace at 207 Bloomfield Avenue in Caldwell serves as a memorial to Cleveland and contains, among other items, the cradle he slept in as a baby. If he were alive, Cleveland might be reluctant to visit his old home because his boyhood was harsh. The future president's father was a stern Presbyterian minister, and his family often lived in poverty. ■

ditional industries shut down in recent years, but they found creative means to deal with the change. For instance, rug weaving was once a prime enterprise in Little Falls. When the main rug company went out of business, its huge old factory stood for years as a boarded-up eyesore. Today, the building has been restored as a condominium complex for couples and small families.

Newark is still New Jersey's largest city, and it remains beset with large problems. In 1930, almost 500,000 people lived in Newark; sixty years later the city's population had dwindled to about 275,000. Fear of crime forced just about everyone who could afford to move to flee to safer suburbs. Remaining in Newark are the poor, the street gangs, and rows of empty buildings with shattered windows. Yet some neighborhoods are working with the police to combat crime. The Prudential Insurance Company maintains its headquarters downtown. The New Jersey Performing Arts Center, opened in 1997, attracts theatergoers and music lovers. These developments have sparked a lively debate about Newark's future. Some say the city will enjoy a rebirth, while others maintain it will never recover from the 1967 riots. Only time will determine the path of this once-great New Jersey city.

Opposite: Newark is the state's largest city.

The Seeing Eye, a Morristown Institution

Sit on a park bench in Morristown and you are sure to see blind people walking the streets aided by their Seeing Eye dogs. Both the dogs and the people are in training at The Seeing Eye, Inc., which operates just outside of town. The streets of Morristown are a training ground. Guide-dog users and their dogs have to work together for at least three weeks before they become permanent partners. The Seeing Eye, the first guide-dog school in the United States, was established in 1929. ■

The Northwest

Northwestern New Jersey is an attractive area dotted with lakes, historic towns, and farms. However, problems stem from its loveliness. An increasing number of families moving from overcrowded cities are building homes in this country setting. The section's recent popularity is causing traffic jams and ragtag highway development. Long-time residents of the northwest hope some sort of balance will be found between growth and the preservation of the old rural way of life.

During the Revolutionary War, George Washington and his troops spent two winters in the historic town of Morristown. The mansion of Colonel Jacob Ford, where Washington spent the winter of 1779–1780, is now a museum. About 6 miles (10 km) outside of town is Jockey Hollow, where 10,000 of Washington's troops wintered. Model huts built at Jockey Hollow demonstrate how Washington's troops lived, jammed together with twelve men to a hut no larger than a one-car garage. Morristown has a clean and prosperous look. Its real-estate values are among the highest in the state. A tiny park, laid out in 1715, dominates the center of town.

Dover began in the early 1800s as an iron-mining town. It was once called "the Pittsburgh of New Jersey." The iron mines closed in the 1950s, but now a host of alternate industries keep the town busy. In the 1940s, the federal government urged Puerto Ricans to come to Dover and serve as farm workers. Descendants of those Puerto Ricans are prominent Dover citizens today, and the town holds a lively Hispanic festival every Labor Day.

The village of Green Pond is a collection of houses clustered around a beautiful lake. Development in recent years typifies the northwestern section. Until the 1960s, the houses of Green Pond were cabins, used primarily as summer getaways by families from the East. Few of the cabins had insulation to fend off winter chills. So, in winter months, the population of Green Pond fell just like the temperature. Today, most Green Pond homes are winterized and residents stay year-round. Growing communities such as Green Pond are common in this desirable New Jersey locale.

Downtown Newton looks like a throwback to the 1800s. Elegant century-old buildings line its main street. The past is preserved in the Newton Fire Museum, which displays an 1863 hand-pumped fire wagon. The northwestern New Jersey town of Vernon is tucked in the middle of a charming mountain setting. In the winter, Vernon is a magnet for skiers. To the south is Millbrook, a restored nineteenth-century village. Visitors at Millbrook can watch a blacksmith at work over a fiery anvil. The blacksmith was an important worker in farming villages of old, but on hot days his work was drudgery. Millbrook guests can also peer in on an old-time shoemaker at work.

U.S. president
James Garfield

Opposite: Asbury
Park, one of many
communities along
the Jersey Shore

Central New Jersey

Another fast-growing region is the central part of the state. To the west lies Delaware River farm country, while resort towns dot the Jersey Shore to the east. In between lie the lofty forests of the Pine Barrens. These varying landscapes make central New Jersey one of the state's most diverse regions.

Two historic Jersey Shore resort towns are Long Branch and Asbury Park. Long Branch is remembered, sadly, for a long-ago guest. In the summer of 1881, President James Garfield was taken to Long Branch. He had been shot weeks earlier by a deranged man. His doctors hoped the sea air of Long Branch would help the president regain his strength, but the remedy did not work. Garfield died of his wounds while staying at the Jersey Shore.

A few miles south is Asbury Park. Like many other Jersey Shore towns, Asbury Park has a "boardwalk," a wooden walkway raised above the sands. The walkway allows people to stroll along the beach without getting sand in their shoes. Atlantic City's boardwalk is more famous, but Asbury Park's is just as much fun.

Saltwater Taffy

Stores selling souvenirs, ice cream, and candy line the boardwalks of New Jersey's seaside towns. A favorite item for sale is saltwater taffy. Saltwater taffy was developed on the Jersey Shore sometime in the 1870s.

Taffy lovers claim the saltwater variety has an especially tangy taste. But check with your dentist before you bite into this chewy Jersey Shore treat—it has been known to pull the fillings right out of people's teeth.

Ingredients:

2	tablespoons butter, plus butter to grease pans
2	cups sugar
1	cup light corn syrup
1	cup cold water
$1\frac{1}{2}$	teaspoon salt
$\frac{1}{8}$–$\frac{1}{4}$	teaspoon vanilla, chocolate, peppermint , or other flavoring

Directions:

Butter the sides of a large (2-quart) saucepan. Add the sugar, corn syrup, water, and salt. Cook over medium heat, stirring constantly, until sugar is dissolved. Continue to cook, without stirring, until the mixture reaches the hard-ball stage.

Remove saucepan from heat. Stir in the butter. Add flavoring. Pour into a buttered 10 x 10 x 1 inch pan. Cool until you can easily pick it up, about 15–30 minutes.

Butter hands and then pull the taffy until it becomes difficult to pull. Divide the taffy into four or five parts. Pull each piece into a long strip, about half an inch thick, and with scissors or a sharp knife cut the taffy into small pieces.

Wrap each piece individually in cellophane.

Princeton, home of Princeton University, is one of New Jersey's very special towns. It was founded in the 1690s by Quakers. Today's visitors walk the grounds of the Princeton Battlefield State Park, site of an important Revolutionary War engagement, where a 250-year-old farmhouse serves as a museum. The university, with its pleasant tree-lined streets, dominates Princeton. Several large corporations, including RCA, have laboratories in Princeton to conduct scientific research.

Farm country stretches across the central part of the state near the Delaware River. Rich soil and plentiful rain make this region one of the most productive farmlands in the nation. Towns developed here centuries ago as trading posts and markets for the nearby farms. In downtown Hopewell stands Railroad Place, an 1876 railroad station now converted to small shops and restaurants. Milford was once a ferryboat station where people and farm wagons were ushered across the Delaware River. Today, Milford is a charming village, known for its antiques shops.

Princeton University

"The Crime of the Century"

In 1927, aviator Charles Lindbergh stunned the world by flying the Atlantic Ocean alone, the first pilot to accomplish that feat. A shy man, Lindbergh retired with his wife, Anne, to a farm at Hopewell to escape publicity. In 1932, the couple's two-year-old son was kidnapped and murdered. An unemployed carpenter named Bruno Hauptmann was found guilty and executed for what headlines called "The Crime of the Century." For years afterward, Hopewell residents complained about the rude reporters and photographers who descended on their town during that tragic time. One photographer jumped on the running board of the Lindberghs' car to snap a picture of the grieving couple. ■

Rising above downtown Trenton is the golden dome of the state capitol. Construction began on this structure in 1792. It is the second-oldest state capitol in the nation. Trenton was founded in the early 1700s by William Trent, who at first called it Trent's Town. Trent's house, built in 1719, is the oldest structure in the capital. The Trenton Battle Monument, a famous landmark, includes a heroic-looking statue of George Washington. The monument celebrates Washington's victory in the Battle of Trenton. Some historians claim the 1776 Battle of Trenton was the most important ever fought by U.S. forces.

The South

The southern third of the state contains farms, a few cities, and miles and miles of seashore. It is sparsely populated compared with the regions farther north. New Jersey families and out-of-state tourists use the south as a vacation land.

"On the boardwalk in Atlantic City. . . ." These words from an old song hail Atlantic City as the greatest tourist town in the United States. It was the first sizable American town devoted entirely to pleasure. In 1891, the city

Casinos dominate present-day Atlantic City.

boasted an amusement park with a wooden "Observation Roundabout," the grandfather of the Ferris wheel. The Miss America beauty contest was first held in Atlantic City in 1921, and the pageant has been an institution ever since.

After World War II, however, tourism dropped off. The city's grand hotels became underused and looked seedy. Then in 1976, the state permitted legalized casino gambling in Atlantic City. Because of the casinos, tourism zoomed from 2 million guests a year to 30 million. But gambling has brought a host of complaints. Residents grumble that only the casino owners make money, not the townspeople. Still, people making money on the tourist trade sing the second line of the old song: "On the boardwalk in Atlantic City/ Life will be peaches and cream."

Ocean City is a family-oriented resort with 8 miles (13 km) of beach, a boardwalk that runs 2 miles (3.2 km), and a music pier for summertime concerts. Nearby Stone Harbor has a 21-acre (9-ha) bird sanctuary that attracts more than 10,000 birds during their nesting season.

The beautiful houses of Cape May

The Barnegat Lighthouse

New Jersey's most famous lighthouse stands to the north of Atlantic City in the town of Barnegat Light. Built in 1855, the lighthouse has long been the subject of landscape painters who try to capture the noble old structure with waves breaking in the background and flocks of gulls sailing over its peak. The lighthouse, affectionately called "Old Barney," can be viewed from hiking trails in Island Beach State Park. ■

At New Jersey's southern tip is the town of Cape May. A time-honored seaside city, Cape May has more than 600 houses that date back to the 1880s. The antique houses are delightfully laced with gingerbread decorations on their outside walls. Cape May Point, a neighboring town, has a stately lighthouse built in 1859.

Inland in southern New Jersey is the city of Millville, which has a 200-year history of glassmaking. At Millville's Wheaton Museum of American Glass, visitors examine delicate old bottles and watch glassmakers at work. The town of Vineland, as the name implies, was founded as a grape-growing center. But it was a dentist, not a farmer, who made Vineland grapes famous. Dentist T. B. Welch was a Methodist who objected to his church's practice of serving alcoholic wine during communion services. So he devised a non-alcoholic grape drink for that purpose. Eventually Welch's Grape

Juice became a household name. Nearby Bridgeton dates back to 1686, when a sawmill was built along the Cohansey River. Bridgeton has a well-preserved historic district, including Old Broad Street Church, built in 1792.

Camden is often thought of as a satellite of Philadelphia, the city that lies directly across the Delaware River. But Camden has long had its own independent industries. One industry began in the late 1800s when Joseph Campbell and an associate marketed canned condensed soup and brought Campbell Soup Company into being. Campbell Soup headquarters is still Camden, though many other industries, including a shipyard and a huge RCA plant, left town. By the mid-1990s, 40 percent of Camden's population lived below the poverty level. However, a bright spot is seen in the historic riverfront that faces Philadelphia, where a multimillion-dollar aquarium and an amphitheater recently opened, bringing visitors back to this historic city.

Joseph Campbell opened his soup company in Camden.

The Phonograph, a New Jersey Development

Thomas Edison's first phonograph was a rather clumsy device that played cylindrical records. One day in 1894, a customer came to a Camden repair shop owned by Eldrige R. Johnson and asked him to fix a broken phonograph. As he worked on the Edison-made machine, Johnson had a brainstorm. He decided to build a new phonograph using flat disks rather than cylinders as records. Soon he founded the Victor Talking Machine Company in Camden. The company later merged with RCA to become RCA Victor. Phonographs made by the company were popularly called "Victrolas," and Johnson, once a humble repairman, retired a millionaire. ▪

CHAPTER SEVEN

New Jersey's Government

Bergen County Court-house in Hackensack

ike all the other U.S. states, New Jersey is governed by its constitution. New Jersey's current constitution was written in 1947. Two previous constitutions were adopted in 1776 and 1844. The constitution divides state government into three branches, or departments: the executive department, the legislative department, and the judicial department.

The Government at Work

The executive department is headed by the governor, who is empowered to enforce laws. New Jersey is one of only two states that have no elected lieutenant governor (Maine is the other). The governor, elected to a term of four years, may be reelected but cannot serve more than two terms in a row. The constitution gives the governor the power to appoint important officials such as the state

Opposite: The capitol at Trenton

The State Flag

New Jersey's state flag, adopted in 1896, shows a version of the state seal against a gold background. It also demonstrates the importance the state once placed on agriculture: In the center of the seal is a shield with three plows drawn on its face, and to the right stands the goddess of agriculture, Ceres. To the left is the figure of Liberty. Above the shield is a horse's head, a reminder that 100 years ago the horse was the most important animal on New Jersey farms. ∎

New Jersey's State Symbols

State song: New Jersey is one of only two states (New York is the other) without an official state song, and it's not because New Jerseyites don't like music. Politicians simply cannot agree on a proper song for the state. In 1980, there was an attempt to make Bruce Springsteen's "Born to Run" New Jersey's unofficial rock song, but even that effort failed to meet the approval of the political leaders.

State nickname: Garden State New Jersey's official nickname derived from its many farms. The nickname goes back to early European settlers who were so pleased with the state's fertile soil that they wrote letters to Europe calling their new home a "garden spot." Over the years, New Jersey has had many unofficial nicknames: the Clam State, for the clams taken off its coast; the Camden and Amboy State, after its once-famous railroad; and the Pathway of the Revolution, because of the many Revolutionary War battles fought on its soil.

State motto: "Liberty and prosperity" For more than a century, New Jerseyites used this motto unofficially before it was adopted by the legislature in 1928.

State tree: Red oak New Jersey has twenty varieties of oak. The large and lovely red oak is common in all the states along the Atlantic seaboard. The dogwood is New Jersey's official memorial tree.

State bird: Eastern goldfinch A beautiful yellowish bird with a cheerful song, the eastern goldfinch (below) ranges throughout the eastern United States. It was adopted as New Jersey's state bird in 1935.

State insect: Honeybee No, New Jersey is not the leading producer of honey; that honor goes to Florida. Still, the honeybee, which builds nests throughout the state, was named the state insect in 1974.

State colors: Buff and blue These colors are seen on many New Jersey symbols, including its license plates.

State flower: Purple violet This very common flower is also called the meadow violet.

State fish: Brook trout Adopted by the legislature as the state fish in 1991, the brook trout swims in New Jersey's inland waters and is considered a prize by fishing enthusiasts.

State animal: Horse New Jersey honored its agricultural past in 1977 when it chose the horse as its state animal.

State dinosaur: Hadrosaurus The hadrosaurus was a duck-billed giant that roamed North America millions of years ago. The bones of a 28-foot (9-m)- tall hadrosaurus were found in the New Jersey town of Haddonfield. The ferocious-looking beast was named State Dinosaur in 1991. ■

New Jersey's Governors

Name	Party	Term	Name	Party	Term
William Livingston	Federalist	1776–1790	Robert S. Green	Dem.	1887–1890
Elisha Lawrence	Federalist	1790	Leon Abbett	Dem.	1890–1893
William Paterson	Federalist	1790–1792	George T. Werts	Dem.	1893–1896
Richard Howell	Federalist	1792–1801	John W. Griggs	Rep.	1896–1898
Joseph Bloomfield	Dem.-Rep.	1801–1802	Foster M. Voorhees	Rep.	1898
John Lambert	Dem.-Rep.	1802–1803	David O. Watkins	Rep.	1898–1899
Joseph Bloomfield	Dem.-Rep.	1803–1812	Foster M. Voorhees	Rep.	1899–1902
Charles Clark	Dem.-Rep.	1812	Franklin Murphy	Rep.	1902–1905
Aaron Ogden	Federalist	1812–1813	Edward C. Stokes	Rep.	1905–1908
William S. Pennington	Dem.-Rep.	1813–1815	John Franklin Fort	Rep.	1908–1911
William Kennedy	Dem.-Rep.	1815	Woodrow Wilson	Dem.	1911–1913
Mahlon Dickerson	Dem.-Rep.	1815–1817	James E. Fielder	Dem.	1913
Jesse Upson	Dem.-Rep.	1817	Leon R. Taylor	Dem.	1913–1914
Isaac H. Williamson	Dem.-Rep.	1817–1829	James E. Fielder	Dem.	1914–1917
Garret D. Wall	Dem.	1829	Walter E. Edge	Rep.	1917–1919
Peter D. Vroom	Dem.	1829–1832	William N. Runyon	Rep.	1919–1920
Samuel L. Southard	Whig	1832–1833	Clarence E. Case	Rep.	1920
Elias P. Seeley	Whig	1833	Edward I. Edwards	Dem.	1920–1923
Peter D. Vroom	Dem.	1833–1836	George S. Silzer	Dem.	1923–1926
Philemon Dickerson	Dem.	1836–1837	A. Harry Moore	Dem.	1926–1929
William S. Pennington	Whig	1837–1843	Morgan F. Larson	Rep.	1929–1932
Daniel Haines	Dem.	1843–1845	A. Harry Moore	Dem.	1932–1935
Charles C. Stratton	Whig	1845–1848	Clifford R. Powell	Rep.	1935
Daniel Haines	Dem.	1848–1851	Horace G. Prall	Rep.	1935
George F. Fort	Dem.	1851–1854	Harold G. Hoffman	Rep.	1935–1938
Rodman M. Price	Dem.	1854–1857	A. Harry Moore	Dem.	1938–1941
William A. Newell	Rep.	1857–1860	Charles Edison	Dem.	1941–1944
Charles S. Olden	Rep.	1860–1863	Walter E. Edge	Rep.	1944–1947
Joel Parker	Dem.	1863–1866	Alfred E. Driscoll	Rep.	1947–1954
Marcus L. Ward	Rep.	1866–1869	Robert B. Meyner	Dem.	1954–1962
Theodore F. Randolph	Dem.	1869–1872	Richard J. Hughes	Dem.	1962–1970
Joel Parker	Dem.	1872–1875	William T. Cahill	Rep.	1970–1974
Joseph D. Bedle	Dem.	1875–1878	Brendan T. Byrne	Dem.	1974–1982
George B. McClellan	Dem.	1878–1881	Thomas H. Kean	Rep.	1982–1990
George C. Ludlow	Dem.	1881–1884	James J. Florio	Dem.	1990–1994
Leon Abbett	Dem.	1884–1887	Christine Todd Whitman	Rep.	1994–

Women and the New Jersey Government

In 1993, New Jersey elected its first woman governor, Republican Christine Todd Whitman. There was a time when Whitman could not have been elected governor and could not have even voted because she was a woman. The state's 1776 constitution gave women the right to vote. But in 1807, the male-dominated state government became afraid that women would vote as a group and establish political strength. So the men passed laws stripping away female voting rights. New Jersey women did not regain their full voting privileges until 1920, when the Nineteenth Amendment to the U.S. Constitution gave all American women the right to vote. ∎

attorney general, treasurer, secretary of state, and secretary of agriculture. The governor's appointments must be approved by the state senate.

The legislative branch is made up of two houses of elected officials: a forty-member senate and an eighty-member general assembly. The legislators write new laws and rescind old ones. New laws must be sent to the governor for approval. The governor can veto, or turn down, a proposed law, but the legislature may override that veto with a two-thirds majority vote from each house.

The judicial branch is made up of the court system. Its job is to interpret the constitution and to try civil and criminal cases. The state supreme court, the highest judicial body, hears cases involving constitutional questions. The county courts have been integrated into the superior court system, so all civil and criminal trials as well as appeals are held in the superior court. No judges are elected; all are appointed from municipal to superior courts.

Kenneth Gibson, Mayor of Newark

In 1970, three years after a series of devastating riots, the voters of Newark elected their first African-American mayor. Kenneth Gibson inherited a city with some areas still in ashes from the 1967 upheaval.

Under his leadership, crime finally leveled off. Before Gibson became mayor, the rate of infant mortality in Newark had been among the highest in the United States, so he launched programs to improve the health of Newark's children.

Gibson was unable to solve all of Newark's problems, but he gave the people hope. Gibson served four terms as mayor and was finally defeated in 1986. ■

The division of government into executive, legislative, and judicial branches is called the separation of powers, or the system of checks and balances. In theory, the system prevents one branch of government from gaining too much power because it will always be held in check by the other departments. The federal government is structured in the same manner, as are most of the other state governments.

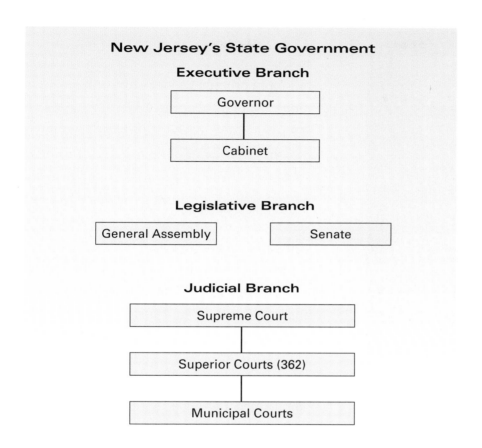

New Jersey's State Government

Executive Branch

Governor

Cabinet

Legislative Branch

General Assembly

Senate

Judicial Branch

Supreme Court

Superior Courts (362)

Municipal Courts

Local governments in New Jersey are administered by its 21 counties and 566 municipalities. The municipalities include communities listed as towns, townships, boroughs, and villages. County governments are called boards of chosen freeholders. That name comes from the days when New Jersey was a colony and only property owners—freeholders—could vote or hold office. Local governments provide for police services, schools, and roads.

Bill Bradley

When he attended Princeton University, Bill Bradley was such an exceptional basketball player that the student body changed the name of the sport—they called it "Bradleyball." Bradley later played pro basketball for the New York Knicks. In 1978, New Jersey voters elected him to the U.S. Senate. Bradley became an astute student of government and one of New Jersey's most famous politicians. He has often been mentioned as a presidential candidate. Bradley retired from the Senate in 1996. ■

Taxing and Spending

In 1998, the state of New Jersey spent $16.8 billion to provide services for its people. The money was used for a variety of needs: to improve roads, to build a new prison, and to pay the salaries of state troopers and other employees. The single biggest item in the budget was $5.3 billion to primary and secondary schools. New Jersey's state-supported colleges cost another $1.4 billion.

Where does this staggering amount of money come from? The largest source of revenue—$5 billion in 1998—came from the state income tax. This is money paid by New Jersey wage earners, usually deducted from weekly paychecks. Sales tax, a tax on goods bought at stores, added another $4.5 billion to the state budget.

Imposing taxes on people is an unpopular task for legislators. It took the threat of a statewide school shutdown in 1976 before the legislature approved the income tax measure. Local property taxes, paid by homeowners, also cause discontent. Less controversial are the so-called sin taxes placed on cigarettes and alcoholic beverages.

State-sponsored gambling is another source of revenue. In 1969, the legislature

Taxes provide money for the police force and other services.

created a state lottery. Community leaders warned that people addicted to gambling would squander family food money on lottery tickets. In 1976, in a statewide vote, New Jerseyites allowed legal casino gambling in Atlantic City. Voters reasoned (correctly, it turned out) that gambling would revive Atlantic City's popularity with tourists. Complaints against state-supported gambling continue. However, the government collects about $1 billion each year from the lottery and from Atlantic City's casinos. Few voters want to discontinue the gambling and risk a tax hike.

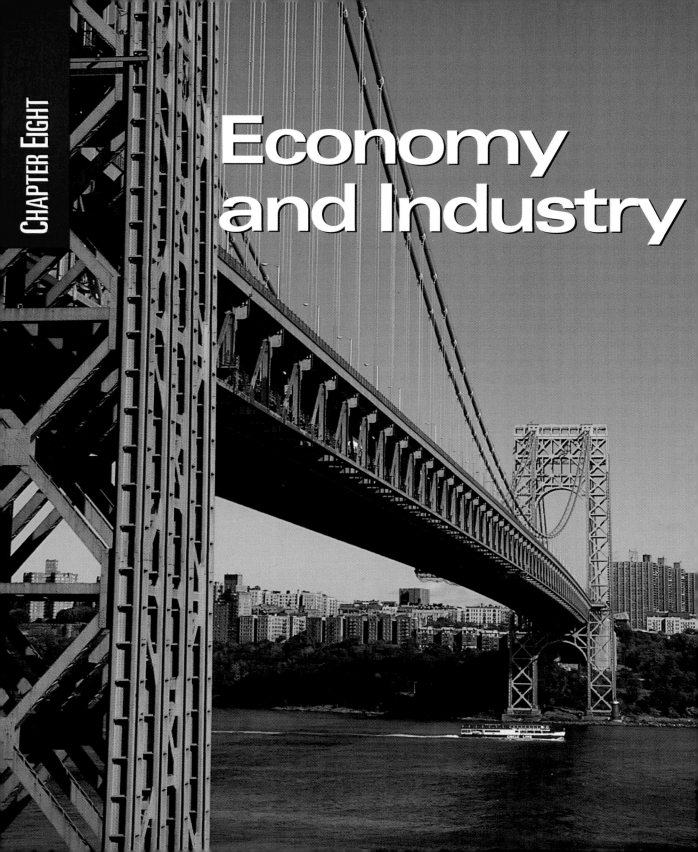

CHAPTER EIGHT

Economy and Industry

Little New Jersey is the fifth smallest in size (total area) of the fifty states. But because of its many factories, it ranks ninth in industrial production. It is also a high-technology state, with more research scientists per capita (per population) than any other state in the United States.

Industries

New Jersey factories turn out $44 billion worth of products a year. Manufactured goods make up 17 percent of New Jersey's entire economic output. Factory jobs account for 25 percent of nongovernment employment within the state. Over the years, the factory base has shifted away from the inner cities to suburban facilities. Still, factories remain vital to New Jersey's economic health.

More chemical products are made in New Jersey than in any other state. Consumer chemical goods include shampoo, makeup, creams, and soap. Factories also make industrial chemicals such as detergents and paint. Pharmaceuticals (drugs used as medicine) are

Johnson & Johnson headquarters

Opposite: The George Washington Bridge, seen from the New Jersey side, connects New Jersey and New York City.

produced by firms such as Johnson & Johnson, Bristol-Myers Squibb, Merck, and Hoffman-LaRoche, which have large research and manufacturing plants in New Jersey. The factories produce life-saving drugs, as well as vitamin pills found in most household medicine cabinets.

Food products are the state's second-leading enterprise. Working closely with the state's farms, canning and freezing plants package fruits and vegetables for delivery to stores. Popular brand-name food items made in New Jersey include M&M candy, Campbell soups, Oreo cookies, Lipton tea, and Budweiser beer. Other factories make bakery goods, soft drinks, roasted coffee, and processed sugar.

In all, New Jersey has about 15,000 factories, employing almost 750,000 people. Additional manufactured goods include printed materials (primarily books and newspapers), electrical equipment, metal products such as cans and screws, scientific instruments, and computers.

Agriculture, Mining, and Natural Resources

Less than 1 percent of the New Jersey labor force is employed on farms. Yet the state's 8,700 farms provide food for millions of people. New Jersey farms rank in the top ten among the states in the output of blueberries, peaches, lettuce, tomatoes, and apples. In the northeast, nurseries and greenhouses grow flowers and shrubs that are sold in New York City florist shops. Northwestern New Jersey has fertile soil for dairy farms. Milk is the state's second leading farm product, after greenhouse produce.

The Hoffman-LaRoche Headquarters

On Route 3 in Nutley, a gate announces the entrance of the huge Hoffman-LaRoche plant. Behind the gate, some 5,000 people work in a complex of more than sixty buildings. Hoffman-LaRoche is a pharmaceutical firm that provides more than thirty-five major medications. Medicines produced in the Nutley facility treat people with heart disease, diabetes, AIDS, and many other serious illnesses. The plant has day-care facilities on the grounds for its many employees with small children. ▪

What New Jersey Grows, Manufactures, and Mines

Agriculture
Greenhouse and nursery products
Milk
Dairy products and eggs
Blueberries

Manufacturing
Pharmaceuticals
Food processing
Printing and publishing
Electrical equipment

Mining
Crushed stone
Sand and gravel

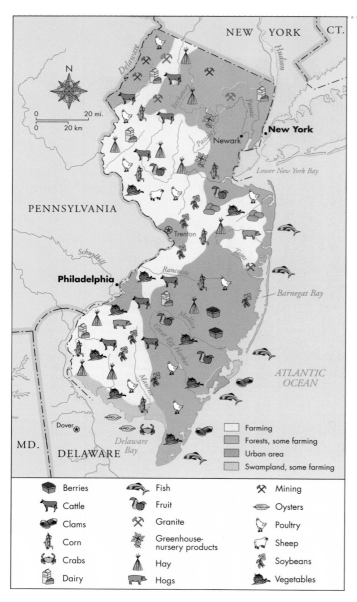

New Jersey's natural resources

Opposite: Farming is an important part of New Jersey's economy.

Berries		Fish		Mining		
Cattle		Fruit		Oysters		
Clams		Granite		Poultry		
Corn		Greenhouse-nursery products		Sheep		
Crabs		Hay		Soybeans		
Dairy		Hogs		Vegetables		

Farming
Forests, some farming
Urban area
Swampland, some farming

Among the materials that New Jersey mines are sand, gravel, and crushed stone, all of which are used by the construction industry. Sand is abundant in the coastal regions, and Sussex County in the northwest is an important source of granite. Mining accounts for only 1 percent of the value of goods made in New Jersey.

Along the coast, the fishing industry remains active. New Jersey, once known as the Clam State, is still a leading producer of clams. The catch off New Jersey's shores also includes scallops, swordfish, tuna, squid, lobster, and flounder.

Lobster trapping off the Atlantic coast

Transportation

None of New Jersey's industrial and agricultural systems could function without the state's network of highways. In 1891, New Jersey was the first state to give money to local communities for road building. Today it has some 34,000 miles (54,717 km) of roadways. State highways are always crowded—every day an average of

Tolls, Paying the Price

The state maintains its highways largely through coins and tokens collected at tollbooths. The tolls raise more than $500 million annually. Motorists grumble about paying tolls. But in 1957, when the Garden State Parkway opened, tollbooths charged 25 cents a car. At the time, a small candy bar cost a nickel. Forty years later, the toll on the Parkway was still 25 cents. However, the price of a candy bar had increased to more than fifty cents. ▪

Commuter traffic on the George Washington Bridge

4,734 vehicles roll over each mile (1.6 km) of highway; the U.S. average is 1,568. But despite this congestion, New Jersey has a better highway safety record than most states.

Each working day, an estimated 200,000 New Jerseyites travel to jobs in either New York City or Philadelphia. New York City is linked to New Jersey by the Holland and Lincoln Tunnels and by the George Washington Bridge, all of which cross the broad Hudson River. Four bridges span the Delaware River to connect New Jersey with Philadelphia.

New Jersey has about 1,200 miles (1,931 km) of railroad track, and some 1.5 million people commute to their jobs via fast commuter trains. Railroads also carry millions of tons of bulk freight such as sand and gravel.

Newark Airport is one of the busiest in the United States.

Newark International Airport is by far the state's busiest. In the 1990s, Newark served 9.7 million people each year, making it the eighth-busiest air terminal in the nation.

Newark and its neighboring city, Elizabeth, are large seaports. Newark and Elizabeth each handle more cargo than New York City. Other port facilities are in Hoboken, Jersey City, and Bayonne. One of the state's most active seaports is at Paulsville, along the Delaware River Bay.

Banking, Finance, and the Service Industry

New Jersey has more than 200 insured banks and savings institutions. Its 100 largest banks have deposits of $90 billion. Insurance has long been a major New Jersey enterprise. In the 1990s, New Jersey cities were headquarters to fifty-six casualty insurance companies and thirteen life insurance companies. The headquarters of Prudential, the insurance giant, stands in Newark.

Service workers are people who provide a service rather than make a product. For example, a plumber is a service worker, as is a store clerk or a schoolteacher. In New Jersey, the majority of jobs available are in the service industry. Travelers visiting the state spend about $22.9 billion each year in hotels, gambling casinos, restaurants, and stores. About 403,000 New Jersey workers are employed in tourist-related businesses.

Shopping Malls, the New Town Squares

Thousands of service jobs are created by shopping malls. The malls are a gathering place, a lot like town squares in older times. The first major shopping mall in New Jersey was built in 1960 in Menlo Park. ■

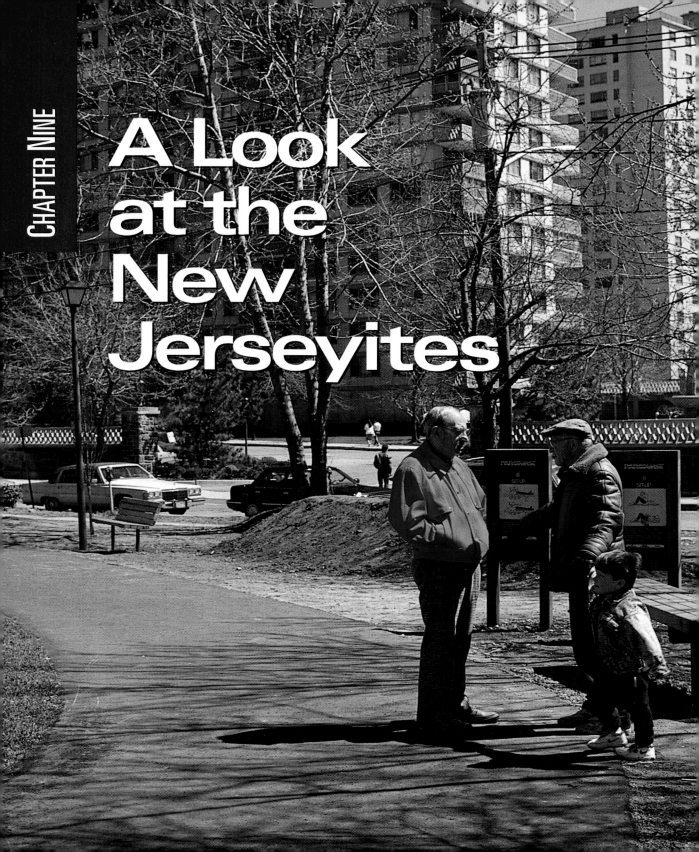

A Look at the New Jerseyites

A state's true wealth comes not from its industries but from its people, and in this regard, New Jersey is blessed. The Garden State enjoys a diverse population with a variety of rich ethnic backgrounds.

Population Distribution

New Jersey is the most crowded state in the United States. An average of 995 people live on each square mile (384 per sq km) of the state's territory. New York, by comparison, has 367 people per square mile (141 per sq km). Also, New Jersey is one of the most urban of all the states—almost nine of every ten residents live in what are classified as cities and towns.

Do these statistics mean New Jerseyites live practically on top of one another in smoky cities where they rarely see a blade of grass? No! The state's population is concentrated in two regions— the northeast, near New York City, and the south-central area near

Opposite: Fort Lee's
Constitution Park

Trenton, Camden, and the towns that lie across the Delaware River from Philadelphia. Fewer people live in the northwest and the south. In those regions, wilderness and farms prevail. With New Jersey's excellent system of roads, families can easily escape the cities to relax in the country.

Population of New Jersey's Major Cities (1990)

Newark	275,221
Jersey City	228,537
Paterson	140,891
Elizabeth	110,002
Edison	88,680
Camden	87,492

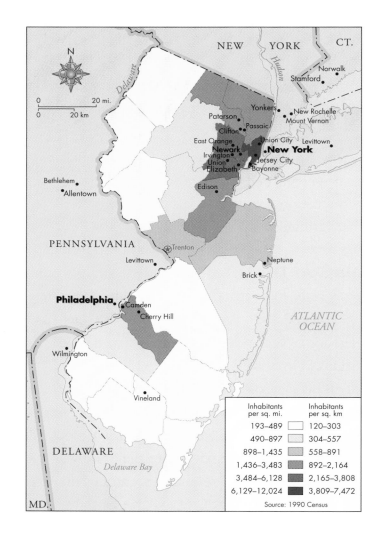

New Jersey's population density

The northeast corner has New Jersey's densest population. Here rise Union City, Jersey City, East Orange (and its cousin towns Orange, West Orange, and South Orange), Hoboken, Elizabeth, and Newark. All these major population centers lie within a few miles of each other and are separated by an ocean of suburbs. Hudson County in the northeast has an average of 12,000 people per square mile (4,632 per sq km). By contrast, New Jersey's sparsest population region is found in Cumberland and Salem Counties to the far south. Salem County holds an average of only

Hoboken is part of New Jersey's most crowded region.

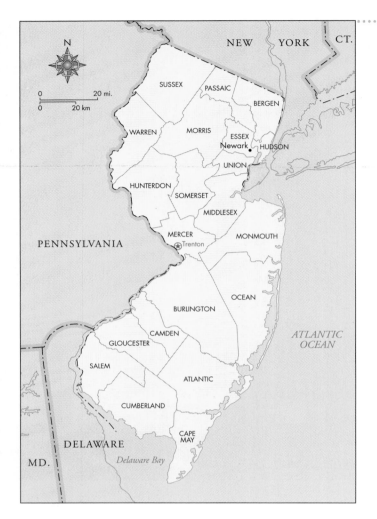

New Jersey's counties

200 people per square mile (77 per sq km). Centre Grove is considered a large town in Cumberland County, but the village would not even appear on a map of the northeast.

Central New Jersey has been the fastest-growing region in recent years, but Ocean County, on the Jersey Shore, saw its population double in the 1980s. No doubt the south and central areas will continue to grow as people seek out the natural beauty offered by rural New Jersey.

Ethnic New Jersey

Want to enjoy food from India? Come to New Jersey, where Indian restaurants abound. Is Indian food too spicy for your tastes? Come to New Jersey, where just about any town has an Italian, German, or Chinese restaurant. New Jersey is an ethnic stew, a place where people from every corner of the world have settled. The people brought along their food, their festivals, and their traditions. One of the fascinations the Garden State offers is its wide variety of people.

In New Jersey's beginnings as a state, English, Dutch, and Germans were in the majority, and the state has always had a large African-American population. At the time of the American Revo-

The Ramapough Mountain Indians

During the Revolutionary War, a group of about 3,000 black and white women were enslaved and then abandoned by the British. The women settled in the Ramapo Mountains of northern New Jersey, where they merged with a band of Tuscarora Indians. Runaway slaves and deserters from the British and Hessian armies joined this mountain society. The people intermarried to form an intriguing ethnic mix that came to be called the "Jackson Whites." Their descendants still live in northern New Jersey, near Ringwood and Mahwah. They now proudly call themselves the Ramapough Mountain Indians.

lution, New Jersey had more African-Americans than any other northern state except New York. Early in the twentieth century, a flood of immigrants from southern and eastern Europe arrived. After World War II, a fresh wave of immigrants came from Asia and Latin America.

Today, New Jersey's population is predominantly Caucasian and African-American. Puerto Ricans are the fastest-growing Hispanic group. The 1960 census counted 55,000 Puerto Ricans in New Jersey; by 1990 that figure had zoomed to 220,000. The largest group of Asians come from India. Almost 1 million New Jerseyites were born in foreign countries. Italy, Cuba, and India are the leading home countries for today's foreign-born residents.

New Jersey's religious makeup reflects its diverse population. Roman Catholics are the most prevalent, with about 3.2 million followers. Other major Christian groups include Methodists, Presbyterians, Episcopalians, Lutherans, and Baptists. Almost 500,000 Jews live in New Jersey.

People of all races live and work together in the Garden State.

Children aged six through fifteen are required to attend school.

Education

Historically, the schoolroom is a meeting place of different cultures. In schools, children of various backgrounds study together and learn to live in harmony.

New Jersey law states that all children must attend school from ages six through fifteen. New Jersey has 2,147 elementary schools and 666 secondary schools. The total school enrollment (elementary and secondary combined) is 1.1 million. Each year, New Jersey spends about $9,600 per pupil, one of the highest rates of student expenditure in the United States.

The state's most prestigious universities are Princeton in the town of Princeton and Rutgers in New Brunswick. Both universities date back to colonial times. Two Princeton graduates signed the U. S. Declaration of Independence. Other major universities include Fairleigh Dickinson in Teaneck; Seton Hall in South Orange; and Drew University in Madison. About 342,000 full-time and part-time college students are enrolled in classes throughout the state.

CHAPTER TEN

The World of Art and Entertainment

Sports are important to many New Jersey residents.

New Jersey has long been a home for artists and writers, and lively theater groups perform in its cities today. Its sports fans are loud and full of passion. An active world of entertainment makes the Garden State an exciting place for residents and visitors alike.

A Proud Literary Tradition

"Out of the Cradle Endlessly Rocking" is a poem that tells of a little boy studying a mockingbird who is mourning its dead mate. The bird's song teaches the boy that death is simply a part of the cycle of life. The poet is Walt Whitman, who believed it was his duty to lead souls to God. For the last twenty years of his life, Whitman lived and worked in Camden. A series of Whitman's poems called "Drum Taps" describes the horror and sadness he saw during the Civil War.

Anne Morrow Lindbergh was famous mainly as the wife of aviator Charles Lindbergh. But Anne, who was born in Englewood,

Opposite: Skyland Manor, Ridgewood

Judy Blume grew up in Elizabeth.

was an accomplished writer. Her book *Gift from the Sea* (1955) studies the meaning of life for women.

William Carlos Williams of Rutherford worked as a baby doctor during the day and wrote powerful poetry at night. In 1963, Williams won the Pulitzer Prize for poetry. His long poem "Paterson" gives a moving description of that New Jersey city.

Modern New Jersey writers talk to children and speak to the stars. The late Carl Sagan grew up in Rahway and spent his boyhood peering through telescopes. A brilliant astronomer and writer, Sagan wrote about complex movements of heavenly bodies in a way that readers found both interesting and understandable. Writer Judy Blume grew up in Elizabeth. Her stories such as *Are You There God? It's Me Margaret* and *Tales of a 4th Grade Nothing* are beloved by kids. She has also written three novels for adults. Another writer of books for young people was Harriet Adams of Maplewood. Under the pen name Carolyn Keene, Adams created the wildly popular Nancy Drew mystery series.

Music and Theater

Jazz clubs operate in northern New Jersey and in seaside resorts such as Asbury Park, while rock and the best in popular music are performed at the PNC Banks Art Center in Holmdel. World-class music and dance are presented at McCarter Theater Center of the

Diners, a New Jersey Treat

After a concert, New Jerseyites drive to their favorite diner for a late-night meal. Diners are roadside restaurants that became popular on the East Coast during the 1930s. Some early diners were made of surplus railroad cars cemented to the ground. With more than 2,000 such restaurants, New Jersey is hailed as "the diner capital of the world."

Diners are often run by Greek or Italian proprietors, and many families have a favorite diner where they know the proprietor by his or her first name. New Jersey diners tend to specialize in seafood. Old and famous Garden State diners include Chappy's in Paterson, Olga's in Marlton, the Summit in Summit, the Tick Tock in Clifton, and Tom's in Ledgewood. ■

The Newark Museum

The Newark Museum in downtown Newark is one of the state's finest. Many splendid examples of American paintings and sculpture are on display, and New Jersey artists predominate in its sculpture garden. Also there is the Old Stone Schoolhouse, a 1784 structure that was moved to the museum. An exhibit of old firefighting equipment is a highlight of this popular Newark attraction. ■

Performing Arts in Princeton. The New Jersey Symphony Orchestra gives more than 150 concerts in various towns each year. Ballet companies include the Garden State Ballet (Newark), the New Jersey Ballet Company (West Orange), and the Mount Laurel Regional Ballet Company (Mount Laurel).

Theater groups large and small attract enthusiastic audiences. The Paper Mill Playhouse in Millburn puts on musicals, dramas, and children's theater. Montclair has a popular small theater com-

The New Jersey Performing Arts Center opened in Newark in 1997.

Monuments to Whitman

At age fifty-five, Walt Whitman was crippled by a stroke. He went to Camden to live with his brother and spent the happiest and most productive years of his life there. His house is preserved as part of the state-supported Whitman House and Library. Lovers of his work visit the Whitman tomb at Camden's Harleigh Cemetery. The tomb bears an inscription of Whitman's words reflecting his belief in death and afterlife: "For that of me which is to die." ■

pany, and the New Jersey Shakespeare Festival meets at Drew University in Madison. New Brunswick is also a center of theater activity. The George Street Playhouse presents old and beloved plays, as well as new works by unknown writers. The State Theater hosts musical numbers and stand-up comics. New Brunswick's Crossroads Theater is dedicated to presenting works on the African-American experience.

The state's newest dramatic arts enterprise is the New Jersey Performing Arts Center, which opened in 1997 in Newark. Its mission, according to a state spokesperson, is "to serve as a host to the world's best performing artists and as a home to New Jersey's best companies. . . ." The center is a complex of buildings that features a 2,700-seat theater. Built in the middle of downtown Newark, the Performing Arts Center will draw the theatergoing public and help to revive a troubled city.

Entertainers Born in New Jersey

Countless singers and movie stars were born in the Garden State. A partial list includes the following:

Whitney Houston (Newark): One of the nation's top vocalists (above).

Jack Nicholson (Neptune): Winner of the Academy Award as Best Actor for *One Flew Over the Cuckoo's Nest* (1975) and *As Good As It Gets* (1997) and Best Supporting Actor in *Terms of Endearment* (1983).

Joe Pesci (Newark): After working for years as a stand-up comic in New Jersey nightclubs, Pesci got a start in the movies by taking gangster roles; he won the Academy Award as Best Supporting Actor for his performance in *GoodFellas* (1990).

Paul Simon (Newark): With partner Art Garfunkel, performed "Mrs. Robinson" and other unforgettable songs in the 1960s.

Meryl Streep (Summit): An accomplished movie actress, Streep won the Academy Award as Best Actress for *Sophie's Choice* (1982).

Dionne Warwick (East Orange): Songs such as "Promises, Promises" and "What the World Needs Now" have made Warwick a beloved vocalist.

Frank Sinatra (Hoboken): Known as "Old Blue Eyes," Sinatra (below) was a popular singer starting in the 1940s. ■

The Ringwood Manor, an Architectural Jewel

New Jersey has many houses and buildings that are treasured for their history as well as their architecture. One such building is the Ringwood Manor, which rises above Ringwood State Park in Passaic County. The grounds were an important ironworks during the Revolutionary War. General George Washington visited Ringwood many times. The mansion, improved upon by several families between 1810 and 1930, is now a historic landmark. ■

The Fine Arts

In colonial America, women were supposed to stay at home, cook, and rear children. Their artistic leanings were confined to "womanly chores" such as sewing. One colonial woman, Patience Lovell Wright from Bordentown, broke the rules. A widow with three young children, she traveled to England in 1772 to study the art of sculpture. Wright fashioned a full-size wax figure of the British dignitary William Pitt, which still stands at London's Westminster Abbey.

In the 1800s, George Inness of Montclair rose to become one of the nation's finest landscape painters. Inness loved to take his easel out in the country and paint nature as he saw it. He was particularly charmed by cloud formations and the sky. The very scenic Delaware Water Gap was one of Inness's favorite places to paint. Some of his finest works now hang in the Montclair Art Museum.

The state supports a large colony of working artists including sculptor George Segal of South Brunswick, famous for his "plastic people." Gregorio Prestopino of Roosevelt is a widely recognized painter whose work appears in the finest galleries, while George Tice, a photographer from Iselin, is renowned for his portraits of Amish people. Leading New Jersey art museums include the Montclair Art Museum in Montclair, the Noyes Museum in Oceanville, and the Princeton Art Museum in Princeton.

Sports

At one time, Garden State fans had to content themselves with cheering for New York City teams, such as baseball's Yankees and basketball's Knicks. Today, the state boasts its own professional teams: hockey's New Jersey Devils (named after the state's famous "devil" legend) and basketball's New Jersey Nets. Pro football's Giants and Jets play their home games in Giants Stadium at the Meadowlands. Those two teams were once based in New York City and moved their games to New Jersey years ago. Despite the teams'

Paul Robeson (1898–1976)
Born in Princeton, Paul Robeson first hit the national scene as a football star for Rutgers. He later became a distinguished singer and Shakespearean actor. Robeson's father was a former slave. All his life Paul Robeson was a bitter critic of racial injustice in the United States. He lost his popularity as an actor when he declared himself a Communist. ■

Sports History, Made in New Jersey

The first recorded baseball game took place in Hoboken on June 19, 1846, when a team called the Knickerbockers met another team called the New Yorks. The game lasted four innings and the New Yorks won 23 to 1. On November 6, 1869, the nation's first intercollegiate football game was played at New Brunswick between the Rutgers and Princeton squads. For that first game, each team was made up of 25 members. The players probably outnumbered the spectators. Rutgers won 6 to 4. ■

New Jersey base, sports announcers continue to refer to them as the New York Giants and the New York Jets. Why? Unfortunately New Jersey still lives in the shadow of the big city to the north.

High-school football and basketball are followed by thousands of cheering fans in the Garden State. Tennis courts abound. Old-time tennis players still talk about Althea Gibson, who lives in East Orange. Gibson, an African-American, dominated woman's tennis in the 1950s when few blacks played the game. Soccer is the favorite sport among New Jersey's huge foreign-born population. In the 1970s and early 1980s, the New York Cosmos played in New Jersey. This professional soccer team featured the legendary Brazilian star Pelé. Today, the New Jersey MetroStars are a leading franchise in the Major League Soccer.

Sports, entertainment, and the fine arts are among the pleasures awaiting the New Jersey visitor. Many people enter the state thinking of negative images: It's a road not a state; it's crowded; it's too industrialized. But a thorough visit to New Jersey quickly proves those images to be false. Get off the turnpike and travel the back roads. Discover the charms of the Surprising State.

Timeline

United States History

1607 The first permanent British settlement is established in North America at Jamestown.

1620 Pilgrims found Plymouth Colony, the second permanent British settlement.

1776 America declares its independence from England.

1783 Treaty of Paris officially ends the Revolutionary War in America.

1787 U.S. Constitution is written.

1803 Louisiana Purchase almost doubles the size of the United States.

1812–15 U.S. and Britain fight the War of 1812.

1861–65 The North and South fight each other in the American Civil War.

New Jersey State History

1524 Explorer Giovanni da Verrazano sails along the coast of New Jersey.

1609 Henry Hudson lands in what is now New Jersey.

1676 British colony of New Jersey is divided into East Jersey and West Jersey.

1702 The two Jerseys are united into a royal colony.

1776–80 Major battles in the American Revolution are fought in New Jersey

1787 New Jersey becomes the third state when it ratifies the U.S. Constitution.

1790 Trenton is chosen as the state capital

1807 Women lose the right to vote that ha been guaranteed in the 1776 state constitution.

1844 New Jersey adopts its second state constitution.

United States History

The United States is **1917–18** involved in World War I.

Stock market crashes, **1929** plunging the United States into the Great Depression.

The United States **1941–45** fights in World War II.

The United States becomes a **1945** charter member of the United Nations.

The United States **1951–53** fights in the Korean War.

The U.S. Congress enacts a series of **1964** ground-breaking civil rights laws.

The United States **1964–73** engages in the Vietnam War.

The United States and other **1991** nations fight the brief Gulf War against Iraq.

New Jersey State History

1876 Thomas A. Edison begins his research laboratory in Menlo Park.

1911 Governor Woodrow Wilson enacts many state reforms.

1927 The Holland Tunnel is completed, creating a road link between New York City and Jersey City.

1945 Rutgers University officially becomes the State University of New Jersey.

1947 The third state constitution is adopted.

1952 New Jersey Turnpike opens.

1969 New Jersey begins its state lottery.

1976 New Jersey institutes a state income tax.

1976 Casino gambling begins in Atlantic City.

1993 Christine Todd Whitman is elected the first woman governor of New Jersey.

Fast Facts

State capitol

Statehood date	December 18, 1787, the 3rd state
Origin of state name	Named by the Duke of York after England's Isle of Jersey
State capital	Trenton
State nickname	Garden State
State motto	Liberty and Prosperity
State bird	Eastern goldfinch
State flower	Purple violet
State dinosaur	Hadrosaurus
State animal	Horse
State shell	Knobbed whelk
State folk dance	Square dance
State insect	Honeybee
State song	None

The Palisades

Newark

Young athletes

State tree	Red oak
State fair	Cherry Hill (August)
Total area; rank	8,215 sq. mi. (21,277 sq km); 46th
Land; rank	7,419 sq. mi. (19,215 sq km); 46th
Water; rank	796 sq. mi. (2,062 sq km); 33rd
Inland water; **rank**	371 sq. mi. (960 sq km); 39th
Coastal waters; **rank**	425 sq. mi. (1,102 sq km); 13th
Geographic center	Mercer, 5 miles (13 km) southeast of Trenton
Latitude and longitude	New Jersey is located approximately between 41° 20' and 39°N and 76° 30' and 74° W.
Highest point	High Point, 1,803 feet (550 m)
Lowest point	Sea level along Atlantic Ocean
Largest city	Newark
Number of counties	21
Longest river	Raritan River, 75 miles (121 km)
Population (rank)	7,748,634 (1990); 9th
Density	995 persons per sq. mi. (384 per sq km)
Population distribution	89% urban, 11% rural

**Ethnic distribution
(does not equal 100%)**

White	79.31%
African-American	13.41%
Hispanic	9.57%
Asian and Pacific Islanders	3.53%
Native American	0.19%
Other	3.56%

Garden at Ringwood Manor

Record high temperature	110°F (43°C) at Runyon on July 10, 1936
Record low temperature	−34°F (−37°C) at River Vale on January 5, 1904
Average July temperature	75°F (24°C)
Average January temperature	31°F (−1°C)
Average yearly precipitation	45 inches (114 cm)

New Jersey's Natural Areas

National Recreation Areas and Scenic Trails

The Delaware Water Gap is a scenic and historic area along the New Jersey–Pennsylvania border.

The Appalachian Trail passes through the length of New Jersey. The trail is 2,158 miles (3,473 km) long and stretches from Maine to Georgia.

The Delaware Water Gap

National Historical Park and Sites

Edison National Historic Site (West Orange) contains Thomas A. Edison's home, laboratories, and research facilities.

Morristown National Historical Park houses the winter quarters of the Continental Army.

National Monuments

Statue of Liberty National Monument is located in both New York and New Jersey. It has become an international symbol of freedom and liberty.

High Point State Park

State Parks

New Jersey has 40 state parks and 11 state forests, including *Liberty State Park*, near the Statue of Liberty and Ellis Island. This park has fine views of New York City as well as a first-class science museum.

Sports Teams

NCAA Teams (Division 1)

Fairleigh Dickinson University Knights

Monmouth University Hawks

Princeton University Tigers

Rider University Broncos

Seton Hall University Pirates

St. Peter's College Peacocks

State University of New Jersey–Rutgers Scarlet Knights

National Basketball Association

New Jersey Nets

National Football Association

New York Jets

New York Giants

National Hockey League

New Jersey Devils

Jets wide receiver
Wayne Chrebet

Cultural Institutions

Libraries

Harvey S. Firestone Library at Princeton University is the state's largest research collection.

Newark Public Library is the largest in the state.

State Library (Trenton) has a large law and history collection.

Museums

New Jersey State Museum (Trenton) features exhibits on archaeology, decorative arts, fine arts, and natural history.

Newark Museum includes a planetarium and art, science, and natural-history exhibits.

The National Headquarters of the Boy Scouts of America has public exhibits devoted to the history of scouting in the United States.

Performing Arts

New Jersey has three major opera companies, one major symphony orchestra, three major dance companies, and one major professional theater company.

Universities and Colleges

In the mid-1990s, New Jersey had 33 public and 28 private institutions of higher learning.

The New Jersey Performing Arts Center

Annual Events

January–March

Super Science Weekend in Trenton (January)

Washington's Birthday Celebration in Titusville (February)

Jersey Coast Boat Show in Asbury Park (February and March)

April–June

Archery Classic in Atlantic City (April)

Cherry Blossom Display in Newark (April)

Canoe Races in Howell (May)

Cherry tree

New Jersey Seafood Festival in Belmar (June)

ShopRite LPGA Classic in Somers Point (June)

National Marbles Tournament in Wildwood (June)

July–September

Pathmark Women's Professional Tennis Classic in
Mahwah (July)

New Jersey Offshore Grand Prix Ocean Races in Point
Pleasant (July)

New Jersey Shuffleboard Championships in Ocean City
(July)

Whitesbog Blueberry Festival in Browns Mills (July)

New Jersey Festival of Ballooning in Readington (July)

Hummingbird Extravaganza in Swainton (August)

Flemington Fair (August)

Sussex Country Farm and Horse Show in Sussex (August)

Baby Parades in Avalon, Ocean City, Sea Isle City, and
Wildwood (August)

Miss America Pageant in Atlantic City (September)

October–December

Victorian Week in Cape May (October)

Cranberry Festival in Chatsworth (October)

Grand Christmas Exhibition in Wheaton Village (November
and December)

Reenactment of Washington's Crossing of the Delaware in
Titusville (December 25)

Victorian Christmas Celebration in Cape May (December)

Englewood street fair

Cape May

Frank Sinatra

Famous People

Bud Abbott (1898–1974)	Comedian
Edwin (Buzz) Aldrin (1930–)	Astronaut
William (Count) Basie (1904–1984)	Musician
Moe Berg (1902–1972)	Baseball player
Lawrence (Yogi) Berra (1925–)	Baseball player and manager
William (Bill) Bradley (1943–)	Basketball player and politician
Aaron Burr (1756–1836)	Vice president of the United States
Grover Cleveland (1837–1908)	U.S. president
James Fenimore Cooper (1789–1851)	Author
Stephen Crane (1871–1900)	Author
Mary Mapes Dodge (1831–1905)	Author
Thomas Alva Edison (1847–1931)	Inventor
Malcolm Forbes Jr. (1947–1990)	Publisher
Allen Ginsburg (1926–1997)	Poet
Mary Ludwig Hays (Molly Pitcher) (1754–1832)	Revolutionary War hero
Joyce Kilmer (1886–1918)	Poet and critic
Jack Nicholson (1937–)	Actor
Dorothy Parker (1893–1967)	Author
Zebulon Pike (1779–1813)	Military officer and explorer
Paul Robeson (1898–1976)	Singer and actor
Antonin Scalia (1936–)	U.S. Supreme Court justice
Frank Sinatra (1915–1998)	Actor and singer
Bruce Springsteen (1949–)	Singer

Bruce Springsteen

Walt Whitman

Alfred Stieglitz (1864–1946)	Photographer
Walt Whitman (1819–1892)	Poet
William Carlos Williams (1883–1963)	Physician and poet
Thomas Woodrow Wilson (1856–1924)	U.S. president

To Find Out More

History

- Fraden, Dennis. *New Jersey Colony.* Chicago: Childrens Press, 1991.

- Fredeen, Charles. *New Jersey.* Minneapolis: Lerner, 1993.

- Hansen, Judith. *Seashells in my Pocket: A Child's Nature Guide to Exploring the Atlantic.* Boston: AMC Books, 1992.

- McMahon, William. *Pine Barrens Legends, Lore, and Lies.* Wilmington, Del.: Mid-Atlantic Press, 1986.

- Morrison, Robert H. *America's Atlantic Isles.* Washington, D.C.: National Geographic Press, 1981.

Fiction

- Avi. *Captain Grey.* New York: Morrow Jr. Books, 1993.

- McCloy, James F., and Ray Miller Jr. *The Jersey Devil.* Wilmington, Del.: Mid-Atlantic Press, 1987.

- Rinaldi, Ann. *A Ride into Morning: The Story of Tempe Wick.* San Diego: Harcourt Brace, 1991.

Biographies

- Davidson, Margaret. *The Story of Thomas Alva Edison: The Wizard of Menlo Park.* New York: Scholastic Books, 1990.

- McKissack, Patricia, and Frederick McKissack. *Paul Robeson: A Voice to Remember.* Springfield, N.J.: Enslow, 1992.

Website

- **State of New Jersey**
  http://www.state.nj.us
  A comprehensive guide to state government information and resources

Addresses

- **New Jersey Chamber of Commerce**
  50 West State Street
  Trenton, NJ 08608

- **The New Jersey Department of Commerce and Economic Development**
  Division of Travel and
   Tourism
  CN 826
  Trenton, NJ 08625
  For information on tourism and travel in New Jersey

- **The New Jersey Department of Commerce and Economic Development**
  Office of Economic Research
  CN 824
  Trenton, NJ 08625
  For information about business and economy in New Jersey

- **Office of Public Information Office of Legislative Services**
  State House Room B03
  CN 068
  Trenton, NJ 08625
  For information about New Jersey government

- **New Jersey Reference Services**
  New Jersey State Library
  CN 520
  Trenton, NJ 08625
  For information on the history of New Jersey

Index

Meet the Author

I'm R. Conrad Stein. I was born in and grew up in Chicago. At one time, all I knew about New Jersey was that it lay between New York City and Philadelphia and that it was the subject of many jokes. Then in 1979, I married Deborah Kent, who is also an author of books for young readers. Deborah is from Little Falls, in the northeastern part of New Jersey. Since my marriage, I have visited the Garden State regularly and have traveled its length and breadth. Like millions of other tourists, I was astonished by its beauty and charm. Surely New Jersey is the Surprising State.

To prepare for this book, I increased my travels, making special visits to the capital and to the lovely regions in the south. I read and referred to at least a dozen books. Several books by author John

Cunningham, a New Jersey native who has written extensively on the state, were particularly helpful. I also talked at length with my father-in-law, Gordon Kent, who has worked as a lawyer in the New Jersey court system for more than forty years.

I am a full-time writer of books for young readers. Over the years, I have published more than 100 books, most of them histories and biographies. As a young man, I served in the U.S. Marine Corps and then graduated from the University of Illinois with a degree in history. I also lived for seven years in Mexico. I now live in Chicago with my wife and our daughter, Janna.

Photo Credits

Photographs ©:

Alan & Linda Detrick: 91
Alan L. Detrick: 6 top right, 7 top right, 39 left, 40, 69, 72, 84, 85, 98, 105, 107, 116, 133 bottom
ALD Photo Inc.: 14 (Tony LaGruth)
AP/Wide World Photos: 6 bottom, 54, 134 bottom (Lennox McLendon), 36, 43 bottom
Archive Photos: 93 (Reuters/Hal Brown), 43 top, 121 bottom, 134 top, 135
Beryl Goldberg: 7 bottom, 28, 45, 62 top, 89
Campbell's Soup Co.: 87 top
Carol Kitman: 108
Corbis-Bettmann: 30, 32, 33 top, 34, 49 bottom, 78, 87 bottom
Envision: 80 (Steven Needham)
Gamma-Liaison: 120, 132 top (Fred Charles)
Gamma-Liaison International: 119 (Lewis Bloom)
Gene Ahrens: cover, back cover, 7 top center, 8, 12, 13, 56, 57, 62 bottom, 64, 65, 66, 81, 86, 88, 90, 102, 103, 122, 128, 129 top, 130 top, 132 bottom
H. Armstrong Roberts, Inc.: 79 (J. Blank), 60 (P. Degginger), 6 top left, 16, 49 top, 58, 61, 130 bottom (Ralph Krubner), 6 top center, 68, 73, 111 (W.R. Wright)
Hoffman-La Roche: 101
Johnson & Johnson: 99

Kobal Collection: 42, 71 right, 121 top
Magnum Photos: 94 (Richard Kalvar)
N.J. Picture Collection, Newark Library: 25 (The Star Ledger), 17, 41
New England Stock Photo: 113 (Jeff Greenberg), 71 left (Tony LaGruth)
New Jersey Turnpike Authority: 9, 48
North Wind Picture Archives: 18, 20, 21, 23, 24, 26, 27, 33 bottom, 35
Photri: 15 (Lani Howe)
Sports Photo Masters, Inc.: 124, 131 bottom (Tomasso DeRosa)
Stock Boston: 114, 117, 129 bottom (Jeff Greenberg), 96 (Nik Kleinberg), 106 (Richard Pasley), 97, 109, 133 top (Rhonda Sidney), 63 (David Ulmer)
The Seeing Eye Inc.: 76
Tony Stone Images: 104 (Paula Bronstein), 67 (Laurie Campbell), 2, 131 top (Phil Degginger), 74 (Doris Dewitt), 7 top left, 38 top, 47, 82 (Hulton Getty), 83 (Bob Krist), 75, 129 center (Don Spiro)
U.S. Department of the Interior, National Park Service, Edison National Historic Site: 38 bottom
UPI/Corbis-Bettmann: 118 (J. Smestad), 39 right, 46, 51, 52, 123
Yale University Art Gallery: 31 (Joseph Szaszfai).
Maps by XNR productions